Text and illustrations
David Balade

DESIGNING CELTIC ORNAMENT

Vivays Publishing

Table of contents

p. 4   *Introduction*

p. 12   **SPIRALS AND TRISKELS**
p. 14   *Introduction*
p. 20   The origins of the Celtic spiral
p. 34   Triskels and double spirals
p. 66   Free spirals

p. 78   **INTERLACE**
p. 80   *Introduction*
p. 86   Interlace and trees of life
p. 102   Single ribbon interlace
p. 130   Interlace with animals

p. 150 **LABYRINTHS**
p. 152 *Introduction*
p. 158 Circular labyrinths
p. 160 Medallions with labyrinths
p. 161 Crosses with labyrinths
p. 166 Carpet pages with labyrinths
p. 168 Lozenge-shaped labyrinths
p. 170 Diagonal labyrinths
p. 172 Carpet-page elements

p. 174 **BESTIARY**
p. 176 *Introduction*
p. 182 The eagle of St John
p. 184 Other birds
p. 185 Dogs and wolves
p. 188 Wild boars and deer
p. 192 Horses
p. 194 The ox of St Luke
p. 196 Cows and bulls
p. 198 The lion of St Mark
p. 202 Lions and cats

p. 204 How to draw the motifs
p. 231 Remarkable carpet pages
p. 231 Major dates
p. 232 Map and chronology
p. 234 Glossary
p. 236 Bibliography

Introduction

Spirals, triskels, interlace, labyrinths and stylized animals — there is a wide range of decorative motifs for anyone interested in the world of Celtic design. On the magnificent carpet pages of the Irish *Book of Kells* (early ninth century AD), the Agris helmet (fourth century BC) found in Charente, France, renowned for the beautiful exuberance of its form, and the mirror (early first century AD) discovered in Desborough, England, which is decorated with abstract spirals of a timeless elegance, we can see that over the centuries Celtic artists developed the visual potential of an ornamental repertoire particularly rich in motifs taken from antiquity. Far removed from the aesthetic and rational criteria of the classical Mediterranean world that would exert such influence on Western history, Celtic designs seem to reflect an enigmatic, alternative worldview within the European cultural landscape.

Kilmainham Brooch, silver and gold, eighth or ninth century AD. National Museum of Ireland, Dublin.

Detail of the Battersea Shield, bronze and red glass, 350 – 50 BC (Iron Age). British Museum, London.

The history of Celtic art: an ancient and medieval form

Celtic art made its appearance in the eighth century BC. It emerged in central Europe — a region bounded by southern Germany, western Austria and eastern France — with what is known as the 'Hallstatt' style, taken from the name of the Austrian archaeological site that was the seat of a particularly wealthy and powerful chiefdom. This period corresponds to the beginnings of the Iron Age, an era in which artisans began to use iron — a new material — to produce beautifully crafted objects, such as daggers, swords, jewellery, cauldrons and wine jars. Among the items found in their grave goods are also sumptuous chariots and the first golden torcs, — large neck rings which would continue to be made throughout the history of Celtic art. The Hallstatt culture's decorative repertoire is comprised mainly of rectilinear or circular geometric motifs and a bestiary of bull, cow and aquatic bird figurines. During this period Celtic artists were still influenced aesthetically by the dominant cultures of the Mediterranean: the Greeks, Etruscans, Phoenicians, etc.

Beginning in the fifth century BC, the Celts left their native central Europe and migrated as far west as present-day Spain and as far east as Turkey. This period, known as the 'La Tène' era, saw the affirmation of their artistic style, which archaeologists have classified into three subdivisions (explored more fully in the 'Spirals and triskels' chapter: the vegetal or classical Celtic style, the Waldalgesheim style and the 'plastic' style. After initially copying the Mediterranean decorative vegetal motifs, the Celtic artists gradually moved away from them to create innovative forms of 'organic abstraction', of which the triskel is one of the most recognizable elements. Into this interplay of curves and spirals, they occasionally introduced enigmatic animal faces and shapes.

The La Tène era ended with the Roman invasion of Celtic territory (c. 50 BC). Gallo-Roman art then attempted the difficult task of synthesizing the Celtic imagination with a return to more naturalistic representations typical of the classical model. Nevertheless, Celtic art continued on the periphery of the sprawling empire, across the English Channel, and is referred to as 'insular art' in this context. Ireland and Britain were the crucibles in which the ancient Celtic forms, developed over the previous five centuries on the continent, were preserved. In Ireland this was possible because the island was never conquered by Rome, although the remains of a Roman trading post have been found there, and in Britain because the country was conquered quite late and abandoned fairly early. Designs made with a compass, increasingly complex in form, made possible the use of curved lines and completely free spirals. This type of work is found on helmets and shields, probably intended as offerings to the gods, or on the backs of highly ornate mirrors.

After the fifth century AD, insular Celtic art survived only in Ireland. With the Christian missionaries, who admitted into their ranks the Celtic bards and *filids* – poets and seers who inherited the knowledge of the Druids – Celtic motifs from the pagan world were incorporated into works of art intended to glorify God. The period starting in the seventh century AD is considered to be the Irish Golden Age: the age of the illuminated manuscript, of which the most famous, the *Book of Kells,* is considered one of the masterpieces of the early Middle Ages in Ireland and of medieval European art in general. The influence of the Irish school was felt throughout Europe, from Scotland, Wales, Northumbria and Armorica (north-western France) to Switzerland and northern Italy. During this Golden Age the Celtic artisans and their imitators, following in the wake of Irish missionaries, developed a particularly sophisticated ornamental repertoire, whether on parchment, monumental stone crosses or on precious and semi-precious metals used in jewellery and liturgical objects. The ancient spiral motifs continued to multiply endlessly, and angular or rectilinear designs reappeared in Celtic art in the form of veritable labyrinths. This was also the period when the Celts, with great dexterity, incorporated into their decorative range the interlace motifs borrowed from neighbouring cultures. Between the eighth and tenth centuries AD, with the Viking invasions followed by the establishment of Norse trading posts in Celtic areas, a Hiberno-Viking artistic style emerged, characterized by ever more complex interlace designs.

Gold openwork on a Celtic bowl from Schwarzenbach, first century BC. National Museums of Berlin.

After the twelfth century and the Anglo-Norman conquests of Ireland, Scotland and Wales, the Celtic aesthetic started to fade. Only a few works inspired by the style may be found in the history of north-western art: isolated pieces such as the mysterious Irish 'Brian Boru' harp, possibly from the thirteenth century and expertly decorated with interlace, and a few Scottish crosses of the eighteenth century.

In the second half of the nineteenth century, the creative effervescence of European decorative art rediscovered the traditional Irish and Scottish ornamental motifs. The political and identity claims of peoples of Celtic origin would give impetus to this research into a forgotten artistic heritage. Finally, in the twentieth century, beginning in the 1970s, interest in Celtic art grew considerably, in particular through music, dance, jewellery and visual art. Generally speaking, crafts re-appropriated motifs from the past in order to respond to a new enthusiasm for vernacular cultures, now being rehabilitated against a backdrop of increasing globalization.

Celtic motifs and know-how

The great diversity of Celtic decorative motifs may be explained by the long history of Celtic art and its presence across a territory as vast as Europe itself, but also by the variety of techniques and materials that made their production possible. The oldest Celtic motifs are to be seen on painted, incised or stamped ceramics, metal objects and carved stones found during archaeological digs. The designs on stone may be either engraved or carved in bas-relief. The decoration of jewellery and other metallic objects involved sophisticated techniques, such as lost-wax casting, filigree, granulation, and the inlay of precious stones and enamel.

Medieval parchment was painted with a goose quill or a stylus, adorned with particularly detailed designs drawn using a loupe (small magnifying glass) of glass or rock crystal. Alongside the profusion of ornaments of which some still survive, we can imagine that the Celts also applied their motifs to perishable materials that are long gone, such as wood, leather and textiles.

We are often astonished by the Celtic artists' skill in creating these highly complex motif designs. During the classical Celtic period ceramics painted with vegetal motifs, elegant curves and countercurves exhibited highly flexible handiwork that must have required years of experience. As for the regular spiral and triskel motifs, these were undoubtedly made using a compass, as revealed by the horn tablets which preserved construction diagrams made using that instrument. A number of metal discs from the Gallic period also show great sophistication in the art of the division and subdivision of the circle into multiples of three or five. According to some ancient authors, the Druids had an advanced geometrical knowledge that was close to Pythagorean concepts.

On the illuminated manuscripts of the early Middle Ages, in addition to the compass point marks, one can see on the reverse of the parchment — if light is shone through it — the preparatory grid lines used to produce the highly regular pattern of interlace and labyrinth motifs. Over the centuries, Celtic art increasingly appeared as a particularly learned form of structure.

Bronze knot with enamel inlay, Celtic art, first century AD. Private collection.

With regard to the use of colour in Celtic decorative art, little information has come down to us apart from the illuminated pages of Irish books. We know from classical authors that the Gauls liked to wear colourful garments, that they had tattoos and sometimes even painted their bodies before going into battle. Traces of paint on a number of Irish ornamental crosses suggest that the motifs used on the stone were decorated with colour. Insular art is also distinguished by the inlay of enamels in lively primary colours – chiefly blue and red.

Finally, the illuminated books of the Irish Golden Age offer broader insight into this chromatic world. The somewhat limited spectrum of colours used by the scribes of the period consisted of browns and blacks made from oak gall, white from lead or chalk, yellow from orpiment, red from kermes or minium, green from copper and, finally, blues made from pastel, indigo or lapis lazuli. The latter pigment, of which the only known source at the time was Afghanistan, must have been particularly expensive. These books are, therefore, veritable treasures, even beyond their remarkable spiritual and artistic qualities.

The mystery of Celtic symbols and sacred knowledge

Not only are Celtic motifs notable for their purely aesthetic aspect, but they may be considered fascinating symbols rooted in a particularly rich tradition. Their interpretation requires a great deal of caution, however. Despite advancements in research,

current academic knowledge on the subject remains sketchy.

In the pre-Christian era, these symbols were very likely produced by craftspeople who had been initiated into a form of sacred geometry taught by the Druids. Even if they knew how to write in Greek or Latin, these sages, according to certain classical authors, refused to put into writing their metaphysical and symbolic speculations. The first people to hold this sacred knowledge thus left us with many unanswered questions.

Other sources of traditional culture, such as those of Alexandrian gnosis and Christian scholasticism, or those produced by Daoist China, Vedic India and Sufism, left written records of the interpretation of their sacred symbols, which often bear a strange resemblance to Celtic motifs. Generally speaking, these cultures placed greater value on stylized forms, often derived from geometry, than on faithful representations of the reality around them. The main principle behind their artistic creation was to reveal the hidden beauty of the harmonic structures of the universe instead of imitating its concrete manifestations, which they considered imperfect reflections of a transcendent reality. In light of this understanding, the work of the artist consisted of extending the creative impulse of a *natura naturans* through the filter of his or her reason and the perfect mastery of technique. By presenting us with these unrealistic, ordered and often repetitive forms, the artists and artisans of the traditional world invite us to transcend, without realizing it, the surface of naturally occurring and transient forms in order to approach the essence of creation and discover its permanence.

symbols, we should also consider the fact that they are elements of an entire decorative programme and more generally of a cultural context very different from our own. Their meaning is difficult to grasp through our own way of thinking and our Cartesian frame of reference. It would be a great error to try to determine the precise meaning of a motif as if it were a sign representing a single concept. The Celtic symbol, like any symbol, is instead the basis for an analogical way of thinking, sometimes also described as poetic or enigmatic. As is the case with myths, there are multiple modes of interpretation, each valid within its own context. Symbols fascinate us because they seem to preserve the evocative power of a forgotten European language that goes back to time immemorial.

Celtic illumination

The motifs chosen for this volume are generally taken from three major illuminated books of the Irish Golden Age: the *Book of Durrow*, the *Lindisfarne Gospels* and the *Book of Kells*, the last of which is perhaps the most famous of them all today. Besides these works from more than a thousand years ago, adorned with particularly refined decorations, we also have numerous other books from the same era that are just as interesting but have a slightly more modest decorative repertoire: the Gospel books of Echternach in Luxembourg, of St Chad in Lichfield, north of Birmingham, of St Gall in Switzerland, of St Gatien of Tours (now at the Bibliothèque nationale de France in Paris), of Mac Regol (now at Oxford), the books of Mac Durnan, of Dimma, of Armagh, the Harley manuscript, etc.

First page of the St Chad, or Lichfield, Gospels, eighth century AD. Lichfield Cathedral, Staffordshire.

In addition to a similarity of symbolic forms, Celtic art and traditional arts from other cultures show the same taste for the 'all over' decorative principle, meaning the complete coverage of certain surfaces. When trying to understand the meaning of their motifs and

The Book of Durrow

The *Book of Durrow* (mid-seventh century AD) is a manuscript containing the four Gospels: Matthew, John, Luke and Mark. Written on vellum, the Gospel book is one of the first finely ornamented works of Celtic art. In it the Celtic motifs of the past blend harmoniously with Pictish, Roman and Byzantine decorative elements. It is thought that the *Book of Durrow* was begun in Scotland, in the kingdom of Dalriada, and was finished in southern Ireland at Durrow Abbey. Today it is in the library of Trinity College, Dublin.

The Lindisfarne Gospels

Lindisfarne was a monastery founded by Irish missionaries in Northumbria, in the north of present-day England. The book (seventh century AD) contains very beautiful carpet pages (full-page illuminations) with extremely complex interlaced patterns. Given the proximity of Lindisfarne to the Saxon kingdoms in Northumbria, it is thought that the book demonstrates more particularly a synthesis of Germanic and Celtic elements. It is currently in the British Library in London.

The Book of Kells

Some scholars consider this Gospel book (early ninth century AD) to be one of the greatest masterpieces of early medieval European art. Giraldus Cambrensis (Gerald of Wales), a thirteenth-century historian,

First words of the Gospel of St John, from the Book of Kells, *ninth century AD. Trinity College, Dublin.*

saw in it 'the work not of men, but of angels'. Like the two books discussed above, the *Book of Kells* has full-page illuminations consisting of very fine scenes from the life of Christ: the Virgin and child, the betrayal of Judas, the temptation of Christ and a portrait of St John. The page with the monogram of Christ, the Chi-Ro, based on the Greek initial letters of the name of Christ, is one of the most spectacular works of Celtic illumination. The *Book of Kells* is housed at the library of Trinity College, Dublin.

Portrait of St John on the page preceding the Gospel of St John, Book of Kells, *ninth century AD. Trinity College, Dublin.*

spirals and triskels

Introduction p. 14

The origins
of the Celtic spiral p. 20

Triskels and double spirals p. 34

Free spirals p. 66

Introduction

From the beginnings of classical Celtic art in continental Europe after the fifth century BC, until its last, sumptuous manifestations during the Irish Golden Age in the early Middle Ages, the spiral was the most frequent and most typical motif of the Celtic world. Over the centuries artists developed an infinite diversity of spiral designs, culminating in highly refined forms on materials as varied as metal, parchment and stone. Another characteristic element of the Celtic ornamental repertoire was the triskel. The result of a combined interplay of spirals, comma shapes and other curvilinear motifs, the triskel (also known as the triskelion) emerged as one of the most innovative creations of Celtic art. Even if the Celts were not its sole 'guardians', they turned it into a strong symbol of identity that can be interpreted in many ways.

The spiral: a fascinating ancient motif

The history of the spiral in Europe seems to begin in the Palaeolithic era with ivory rods covered with spiral motifs, which were discovered in Isturitz and in Lespugue in the French Basque country and date to around 12,000 years BC. The spiral could be traced much further back in time, for instance to a bracelet of mammoth ivory around 24,000 years old, found in Mezin, Ukraine, if we consider Greek keys and chevrons to be angular versions of the spiral. We will discuss this further later in the book.

In the Neolithic period, around the fifth millennium BC, the spiral motif often appears on decorated pottery from the Danube valley. This was probably inspired by the ornamental decorations of even more ancient Middle Eastern civilizations, such as the one at Çatal Hüyük.

After the third millennium, in the Mediterranean islands, groups of linked spirals appeared which were carved in larger format on tombstones or on temples, such as the one at Tarxien, Malta. With the advent of the Bronze Age, the interplay of spirals became more and more sophisticated. In the Cyclades archipelago, the whorl motif made its appearance, linking multiple spirals on objects similar to rackets, the function of which remains mysterious to this day. A few centuries later, among the Minoans, spirals evolved into the form of octopuses, bucranes (zoomorphic figures in the form of an ox skull or head) and lilies. They were used on ceramics and in particularly elegant Cretan frescoes. Then, among the Mycenaeans, the spiral motif became abstract once again and was aligned in regular friezes on jewellery, ceremonial vessels and a number of carved columns. Later, artists of classical Greece and Etruria combined the palmette, of oriental origin, with the double S or lyre motif on the bodies of vases and as architectural ornaments – designs which would spread throughout Mediterranean and eastern Europe.

In northern and western Europe, excavations have uncovered fewer traces of spirals, but the objects that do feature this motif are more monumental or are technically highly elaborate. In the third millennium BC, a very rich, graphic array of sinusoidal lines, concentric circles and double or triple spirals appeared on some of the tumuli at Newgrange and Knowth, Ireland. These symbols may constitute a carved record of astronomical observations. In the inner chamber of the tumulus at Gavrinis, Brittany, some of the stone slabs are entirely covered with

Vase illustrated with an octopus design (painted faience) from Knossos, Crete, Late Minoan Period II, 1450 – 1400 BC. Ashmolean Museum, Oxford University.

concentric arcs and circles in a pattern reminiscent of fingerprints. Further north, in Scandinavia, with the advent of the Bronze Age, friezes of filigree spirals of astonishing sophistication adorn swords, discs and gold bracelets. These objects travelled the length of the trade routes and influenced the artisans of pre-Celtic northern Europe.

In the very earliest Celtic art, that of the Hallstatt period (between the ninth and eighth centuries BC), the Celts produced an ornamental style that was largely rectilinear, but punctuated by concentric circles and roundels recalling the circular motifs of Bronze Age Europe. From the fifth century BC, they left their home north of the Alps and began to migrate across all of Europe. During this time, known as the 'La Tène' period, they came into contact with the Greek, Etruscan and Phoenician civilizations, and soon discovered a new way of life.

The culture of wine drinking, for example – their immoderate passion for which is described by classical authors – required utensils (wine craters, *stamnoi*, etc.). These drinking vessels began to circulate throughout the Celtic world, spreading the motifs of the palmette, lotus and lyre friezes used to decorate them (see above). Thus there is significance in the motifs from both historical and artistic perspectives.

Detail of a bronze handle found in the tomb of the Princess of Vix (Bronze Age), sixth century BC. Archaeological Museum of Châtillon-sur-Seine.

The spiral's extraordinary graphic development

Let us now look more closely at how Celtic craftspeople appropriated these spiral motifs. During a new stylistic phase in which the style known as 'vegetal' emerged (between the mid-fifth and mid-fourth centuries BC), Celtic artists copied and incorporated classical Mediterranean vegetal motifs into their decorative art, ultimately transforming them. The spirals of the lyre that clasps the palmette were gradually relaxed and extended in the form of comma shapes. Others became double spirals, recalling the Daoist yin-yang motif. Little by little the palmette gave way to a more exuberant lyre pattern. The addition of eyes or heads to the lyre turned it into a dragon or a mask.

From the mid-fourth century BC, Celtic art developed its own distinctive style, characterized by forms that were completely new in ancient decorative art. This Celtic style, regarded as classical, combined comma shapes, spirals and waves – now freed of their Mediterranean structures – in frenzied friezes covering the full length of torcs and the rounded surfaces of helmets. In the same period, the first hints of the famous triskel motif appeared, born of the interplay of curves and countercurves in the Waldalgesheim style. When the comma shapes and spirals were arranged around a centre, the triskel began to take shape. Eventually it gained independence, becoming a motif in its own right: three spirals caught up in a gyratory movement. From these new, endless curves, oscillating between abstraction and vegetal forms, there emerged strange animals – a style sometimes referred to as 'organic abstraction'.

During the third century BC, the sword style, sometimes characterized as baroque, spread across an area bounded at its extremes by France and Hungary, and ended up completely disintegrating the friezes of waves and spirals engraved on bronze scabbards.

After the first century AD, with the expansion of the Roman Empire into Gaul, the spiral motif in its Celtic form gradually disappeared from the European continent. However, in what is today Britain and Ireland, the Celtic elites resisted the aesthetic of the Roman conquerors, favouring the development of an insular Celtic art that would last through the early Middle Ages. The spiral motifs continued their transformation: the spiral broke up into a sharp angle, then the line began to curl up again at its extremity. Trumpet or fan shapes appeared in the new spaces bounded by these curves, freed from the rigour of central or axial symmetries. At the very beginning of this era, particularly in Britain, these more freely composed spirals thus conferred a rare elegance upon mirror backs and sumptuous shields.

Ireland, after the fall of the Roman Empire and the first Germanic invasions, became the main preserver of Celtic decorative forms. From the sixth century AD, with the island's conversion to Christianity, the Irish Golden Age may be said to have begun. The spiral emerged on a new medium — parchment books — that made possible one of the most extraordinary artistic developments in the history of Western medieval art.

Bronze shield with Gorgon head, found in Olympia, fifth century BC. Archaeological Museum, Olympia. Collection of ancient art and architecture.

In the Gospel books, single or double spirals and triskels were multiplied *ad infinitum*, terminating here again in animal heads composed of leaves, trumpet spirals, *peltae*, etc. These designs eventually covered entire pages, known as 'carpet pages'. Metal objects and carved stone crosses, whether in Ireland, Scotland or Wales, reproduced these daring innovations as far as their materials permitted.

The Viking invasions between the eighth and tenth centuries AD, followed by the Anglo-Norman conquest, marked the end of the spiral that was so beloved by the Celts. Apart from a few isolated examples in the ancient Celtic lands, it was not until the Celtic cultural revival of the nineteenth century that this motif, so closely associated with Celtic art, would reappear.

The spiral: universal symbol of energy and transformation

In the Neolithic cultures of the Danube, the S-figures, spirals and waves arranged in friezes were used mainly to decorate funerary urns and vases, which were sometimes anthropomorphic in design and probably intended for ritual purposes. These motifs could be interpreted as the expression of the regenerative power of life-giving waters. In Malta, during the same period, the spirals carved on megaliths became more elaborate, with foliated outgrowths, while in the eastern Mediterranean, the spiral, terminating in a small head, took on the appearance of a coiled serpent: the life force appears to have been represented through these vegetal and animal shapes. In Sicily in that era, large double spirals, carved like the horns of a ram at the entrance to a cave, appear at times to evoke the giant, searching eyes of a mother goddess who guards the secrets of life and the depths of the earth.

In western Europe, spirals and concentric circles were engraved on the stones of megalithic structures aligned with the path of the stars. According to some theories, double spirals describe the waxing and waning circles traced by the sun across the skies over the course of a year between two solstices. It has been observed, moreover, that at each winter solstice, at a specific hour, a ray of sun lights up the central chamber of the tumulus in Newgrange, Ireland. Built probably to give concrete expression to the idea of a giant earthly womb, the tumuli thus appear to be the symbolic meeting points of earthly and heavenly energies, making them propitious for the regeneration of the participants in the rites practised there.

The symbolism of the double spiral in Asia is better known thanks to the survival of traditional texts. The famous Daoist yin-yang principle suggests a spiral movement of condensation and dissipation, materialization in the physical world and dissolution into spiritual oneness. The spiral becomes the link between the two poles of the universe: earthly and heavenly. The same principle appears to underlie the double helix along the axis of the Indian Brahma-danda, a symbolic axis of the world to which Hermes' caduceus (a staff entwined by two serpents) seems to be heir. After all, Hermes is the messenger of the gods and the one who guides souls to the afterlife. The spiral appears here as a path of hypnotic access between the divine and earthly worlds.

The ubiquity of the triskel, seen as the expression of a 'Celtic soul'

Today the triskel is one of the most recognisable symbols of Celtic identity. It is quite simple to draw if one knows how to use a compass, and has also been found, if only occasionally, in other traditional cultures.

Romano-Celtic bronze appliqué in the shape of a triskel, third century AD. Private collection.

It should be noted that the word 'triskel' comes from the term *triskelës* ('three legs'), which is not of Celtic origin but is Greek. In fact, in the form of three interlocked legs, the motif was the symbol of Sicily — the island known in antiquity as *Trinacria* — and used on its ancient coins. The same design also appeared in the Middle Ages on the coats of arms of the rulers of the Isle of Man. They were nobles of Scandinavian origin whose motto *Quocumque jeceris stabit* ('Wherever you throw it, it will stand') explains the design's shape. It also featured very early in Aegean and Mycenaean art, formed by interlocked comma shapes. Another form of the triskel, the *sam-taegeuk*, may be seen on numerous objects in Korea, where it symbolizes the triad of Daoist origin: heaven, earth and humanity. Finally, in Japan triple spirals made up of comma shapes known as *mitsu tomoe* are common in family emblems.

The Celts, however, developed and used to the full the graphic potential of this original motif, which links a mysterious ternary principle to the force of a gyratory movement. According to historians and scholars of mythology, this ternary principle comes from a predisposition among Indo-European peoples, of whom the Celts are a branch, to structure their mental world into threes. For instance, representations of gods and goddesses with three faces are frequent in the Gallo-Roman era, and recall the three Graces or Fates (*Moirai* in Greece, *Parcae* in Rome), related perhaps to the notion of the fluidity of time: past-present-future. Celtic society was also made up of three social groups: the priestly class of Druids, the warrior class of kings and nobles, and the working class of artisans and farmers. Finally, medieval Irish and Welsh poetry reveals a predilection for ternary rhythm. Other theories, much less well founded, have tried to see in this threefold pattern a representation of the 'three elements'. This hypothesis fails to consider that the Celts would have been more likely to distinguish five elements: fire, earth, water, air and fog!

Much ink has also been spilled debating the question of the 'correct' direction of the gyratory movement of the triskel. Evidence of certain cultural practices in the Celtic world seems to support the idea that the clockwise movement was thought to have a beneficial effect. For example, the sabre dance, a Scottish circular warrior dance, always begins counter-clockwise as a sign of hostility and ends in a clockwise spiral to express victory. Ancient Irish epics recount that, before entering a fortified place, rulers had to present their right side — the unarmed side — and circle the palisades moving in a clockwise direction, to signal their peaceful intentions. The choice of the direction of rotation could have been inspired by observing the path of the celestial bodies in the skies of the northern hemisphere. Be that as it may, in Celtic art the triskels turn in both directions. One might imagine that, depending on the direction chosen, the presence of the symbol could either repel evil spirits on defensive arms (shields) or enhance the combatant's vigour when portrayed on lances and the scabbards of swords. Regardless of the interpretation, one thing is certain: the suggestion of movement, energy and growth remains the same.

The absence of speculative texts on the subject written by the Celts makes it difficult to interpret the meaning of the Celtic spiral and triskel. What can be said is that these shapes of cosmic inspiration are typical of the Celtic aesthetic. Well before the appearance of scientific images illustrating fluid mechanics, the forces of magnetic attraction and the principle of fractal growth, or before satellite photos of cyclones and telescopic images of distant galaxies, the Celts seem to have had an intuitive sense of these lines, curves and spirals that are traced invisibly by a life force at work in our universe, which is in perpetual motion.

The origins of the Celtic spiral

Beginning in the fifth century BC, the Celts established more regular contacts with the Etruscan, Greek and Phoenician civilizations. These exchanges, favoured by commerce and diplomacy, revealed to Celtic artisans a new world of decorative motifs from which they would draw inspiration. Soon they transformed the classical Mediterranean motifs of the lotus, the lyre and the palmette into a repertoire of innovative forms, which were characterized by a certain degree of organic abstraction.

The palmette and the lyre

Diversity of forms

The motifs of the lyre and palmette, found on a wide range of vases from the Mediterranean world, were of particular interest to the Celtic artisans of antiquity. Having copied the patterns, the Celts developed the two scrolls of the lyre into an original interplay of curves that could be the origin of numerous spiral motifs to come in the history of Celtic art.

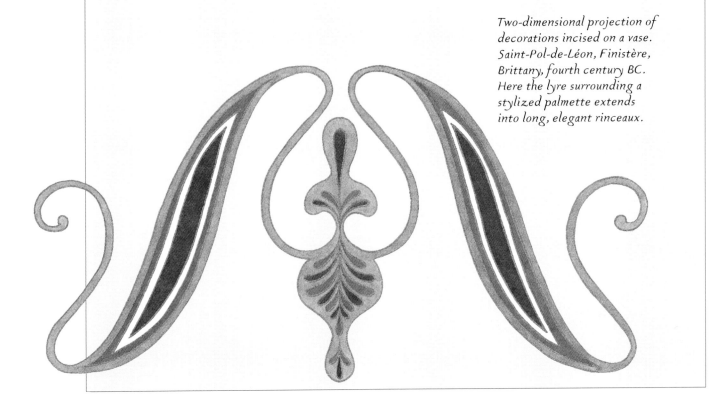

Two-dimensional projection of decorations incised on a vase. Saint-Pol-de-Léon, Finistère, Brittany, fourth century BC. Here the lyre surrounding a stylized palmette extends into long, elegant rinceaux.

Detail of a helmet,
Amfreville-sous-les-Monts,
Eure, France, fourth century BC.
Here the palmette is multiplied
vertically under the lyre.

Ornamentation in bronze,
Mairy-sur-Marne, France,
fourth century BC. Here the
lyres are transformed into
four yin-yang motifs.

Friezes of stylized lyres and palmettes

Diversity of forms

The juxtaposition of the friezes presented here offers a glimpse of the gradual transformation of the motifs of the lyre, palmette and lotus at the hands of the Celts over the centuries. These colourful works enable us to appreciate the structure of the motifs. On the metal objects produced in Celtic antiquity, the structures were sometimes coloured by means of coral or enamel inlays.

Frieze in bronze on an iron helmet, Canosa di Puglia, Apulia, Italy, mid-fourth century BC.

Detail of a frieze on a bronze sword scabbard, Lisnacroghera, County Antrim, Ireland, second century BC.

Frieze in gold repoussé work on a bowl, Schwarzenbach, Saarland, Germany, first century BC (see photo page 6).

*Creation by the author based
on radiating motifs in Celtic
art inspired by nature.*

Bronze disc, Écury-sur-Coole, Marny, France, fourth century BC.

Two-dimensional projection of a torc, Camp de Châlons, Champagne, France, fourth or third century BC. The motifs of the lyre and the palmette cross in a particularly exuberant manner on this neck ring, reserved for the Celtic aristocracy.

Stylized lyres and palmettes

Diversity of forms

By deconstructing the classical forms of the lyre and palmette, stretching and repeating the curves of the motif, and reconstituting the resulting forms according to a central symmetry, the Celts were able to develop an original decorative repertoire marked by a spirit of organic abstraction.

Motif inspired by the gold disc of Auvers-sur-Oise, Val-d'Oise, France, late fifth or early fourth century BC.

Medallions of lyres and palmettes

The evolution of a motif

The motif of the lyre and palmette, generally repeated to form a frieze on ancient objects of Mediterranean origin, has here been transformed and arranged on a circular medallion based on a central symmetry. This original composition suggests some kind of strange flower.

From lyres to dragons

Diversity of forms

The classical motif of the palmette and lyre could be the Mediterranean stylization of the more ancient motif, originally from the Middle East, of the tree of life surrounded by dragons or the 'lord of the animals' holding two serpents. Certain ancient Celtic decorative motifs that extend the lyres into zoomorphic heads recall the theme of pairs of curvilinear animals arranged symmetrically around a vertical axis.

Stylized dragons engraved on a sword scabbard, Varennes-lès-Mâcon, Saône-et-Loire, France, fourth or third century BC.

Decoration on a sword scabbard, Csabrendek, Hungary, fourth or third century BC.

Element of a bronze helmet, Cuperly, France, late fifth century BC.

Belt hook, Holzelsau, Austria, early fourth century BC. The Middle Eastern motif of the 'lord of the animals', flanked by two dragons, is easily recognizable here.

Bronze ornamentation, Saint-Jean-sur-Tourbe, Marne, France, fifth or fourth century BC.

Detail of the Agris helmet, Charente, France, fourth century BC. The ram-horned serpent appears in Europe from the Neolithic period onward. This animal, coiled up like a spring, may embody the life force moving within nature.

Detail of a sword scabbard, Cernon-sur-Coole, Marne, France, late third century BC. This motif, which is reminiscent of a sea horse, illustrates the elegance of the style of sword that spread across the entire Celtic world in the third century BC.

Detail of the Steinenbronn stele, Baden-Württemberg, Germany, late fourth to third century BC.

Detail of a shield, Ratcliffe-on-Soar, Nottinghamshire, England, fourth or third century BC. The tail of this dragon is transformed into a triskel by the interplay of curves and countercurves.

Spirals with stylized animals

Diversity of forms

Alongside the dragons and serpents naturally suggested by curvilinear forms, the Celts sought to incorporate other animals into their motifs, such as birds or horses whose heads harmoniously extend the spirals.

Triskels
and double spirals

From the fourth century BC, the triskel — a design consisting of
three branches with interlocked spirals and propelled by a gyratory
movement — emerged as one of the most characteristic and commonly
occurring motifs in Celtic art. Both in abstract versions and
linked with vegetal and animal forms, the design's full potency
has been expressed over the centuries. Alongside the triskel,
individual spirals continue to exist alone, in friezes
or incorporated into complex decorative
systems.

Emergence of the triskel

Diversity of forms

The triskel motif may have emerged from the curves and countercurves of Celtic variations on the classical lyre motif, the combination of spirals with the wave motif or the disposition of comma shapes around a central axis.

Below: Motif engraved on stone C10 in the inner chamber of the tumulus at Newgrange, County Meath, Ireland, c. 2500 BC. Megalithic tumuli are often thought to be physical representations of the concept of the terrestrial womb. The double spiral motifs engraved on the stones of this site have been interpreted as representing the path of the sun between two winter solstices. This triskel motif here could symbolize the connection between solar and terrestrial life forces.

Right: Painting on a vase, Bussy-le-Château, Marne, France, fourth century BC.

Decoration engraved on a torc, Marne, France, fourth or third century BC. We see the appearance of hidden triskels in the profusion of shapes linked under this palmette.

Decoration engraved on the inside bottom of a bowl, Mintraching, Bavaria, Germany, fourth century BC. This combination of comma shapes gave rise to one of the first triskels in Celtic art.

Triskels and medallions

Diversity of forms

Over the course of time, the triskel became dissociated from friezes and moved away from its vegetal and Mediterranean origins, becoming an independent motif organized by rotation around a central axis. It should be noted that these simple triskels may rotate in different directions.

Detail of a bronze helmet, Apahida, Romania, fourth or third century BC.

Tip of a gold torc, Clevedon, Avon, England, third to first century BC.

Detail of the Killamery
Cross, County Kilkenny,
Ireland, possibly ninth
century AD.

Detail of the South Cross
at Ahenny, County Tipperary,
Ireland, eighth to mid-ninth
century AD.

Decoration on a cylinder lid,
Navan Fort (Emain Macha), Ireland,
second or first century BC.

Aquatic swirls

Diversity of forms

The nuances in the different shades of blue in these triskels suggest the movement of waves and swirling water. Their circular motion, which governs the mechanics of fluids on the earth, is an expression of the Coriolis force. Many galaxies also turn on a central axis in accordance with this same principle of gyratory motion. The triskel thus serves here as a suggestion of these cosmic forces.

Multiple interlocked triskels in a composition inspired by the Aberlemno Cross, Angus, Scotland, early ninth century AD.

Original design inspired by the style of the visual artists of the 1930s Breton movement – known as the 'Seiz Breur' ['seven brothers'] – which linked traditional Celtic motifs with the Art Deco style.

Original design. The triskel opens up into scrolls reminiscent of the flowing patterns typical of Art Nouveau.

Design inspired by the spirals of the Book of Durrow.

Vegetal triskels

The evolution of a motif

By breaking down this motif, we can see how the central triskel is progressively developed with spirals and bouquets of leaves. The triskel thus seems to suggest the principle of a life force, generating forms that expand in space.

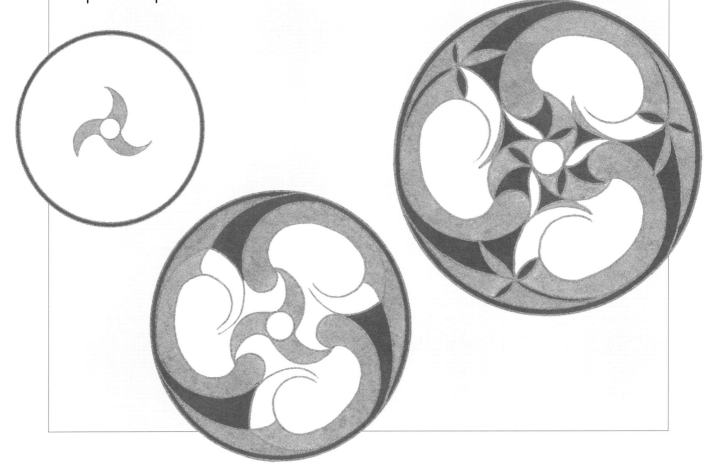

Detail of a door handle, Donore, County Meath, Ireland, early eighth century AD.

Decoration on a horn, Brentford, Middlesex, England, third century BC.

Motif used in the decoration on the inside bottom of a bronze bowl, Saulces-Champenoises, Ardennes, France, fifth or fourth century BC.

Triskels and foliage

Diversity of forms

In these three examples we see how the principle of vegetal growth of the classical lyre and palmette motifs was maintained over the centuries through the triskel, onto which patterns of foliage or plant tendrils were grafted.

Detail of a gold openwork plaque, Phoenix Park, Dublin, Ireland, eighth century AD. The empty spaces filled with black are the author's own design.

Detail of the Donore Disc, County Meath, Ireland, early eighth century AD. It is thought that this disc adorned a wooden object, probably a door.

Triskels and foliage

Diversity of forms

The addition of small leaves to the pre-Christian motif of the triskel is a distinctive feature of so-called 'insular' Celtic art, alongside highly complex animal interlace motifs and labyrinths.

Brooch, Silchester, Hampshire,
England, first century AD.

Detail of a bronze belt buckle,
Lagore, County Meath, Ireland,
eighth century AD.

Motif taken from the
Book of Durrow, *folio 3v*.

Triskels, double spirals and foliage

Variations in colour

With a relatively limited chromatic range, but a particularly rich ornamental tradition, the Irish scribes succeeded in creating a highly diverse decorative repertoire. We can see a number of variations here in the colour schemes of Irish books from the early Middle Ages.

The author's own design, inspired by the Donore Disc, County Meath, Ireland, early eighth century AD.
The ornamentation of the Donore Disc is organized around a central symmetry and the ternary principle of the
triskel, with a mastery that has rarely been equalled. The degree of complexity in the decoration of this metal
object may be compared to that of the 'carpet page' with eight medallions in the Book of Kells.

Motifs with multiple triskels

Variations in form and colour

Detail of the Tara Brooch, County Meath, Ireland, eighth century AD. Queen Victoria was particularly taken with the Tara Brooch, which had been acquired by a firm of jewellers named Waterhouse after its discovery, and she ordered a copy to be made. At the end of the nineteenth century, there was great enthusiasm for Celtic jewellery and for Celtic motifs more generally in Britain. The Arts and Crafts movement, in particular, drew inspiration from the 'insular' Celtic style that was rich in vegetal motifs.

Triskels, interlace and labyrinths

Diversity of forms

As in every classification, we find in the Celtic decorative repertoire hybrid forms that do not fit into rigorously defined categories. Here, triskels blend harmoniously with interlace patterns, crosses and stripes, attesting to the skill and freedom of Celtic artisans in creating their decorative motifs.

Motif engraved in the stone of the Kinnitty Cross, County Offaly, Ireland, ninth century AD.

Medallion from the Book of Kells, *folio 292r.*

*More detail of the Cross page
with medallions from the* Book
of Kells, *folio 33r.*

*Detail of the Cross page with medallions
from the* Book of Kells, *folio 33r.*

Bird triskels

Diversity of forms

Heads of birds with slender, supple necks harmoniously extend the extremities of some triskels. In other ternary compositions the bird's entire body appears, filling the empty spaces within the triskel.

Decoration of a sword scabbard, Obermenzing, Germany, second century BC.

Disc found in the River Bann at Longban Island, County Derry, Northern Ireland, pre-Christian era.

Detail from the Book of Kells, *folio 8r.*

Decoration on a bronze fibula, Ireland, sixth century AD.

Detail of the Donore Disc, County Meath, Ireland, early eighth century AD.

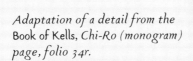

Adaptation of a detail from the Book of Kells, Chi-Ro (monogram) page, folio 34r.

Dragon triskels

Diversity of forms

Beginning with the so-called 'classical Celtic' period and until the early Middle Ages, the heads of indeterminate animals – sea horses or dragons – regularly appear in extensions of spirals and triskels.

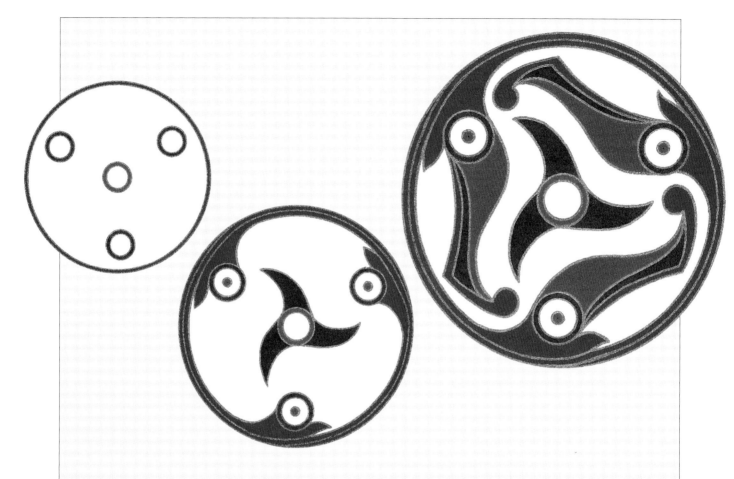

Horse triskels

The evolution of a motif

On refined objects from the Donore hoard, the curve and countercurve
motifs linked to some of the triskels suggest stylized horse heads.

Detail of a door handle, Donore, County Meath, Ireland, early eighth century AD.

Crosses with spirals and triskels

Diversity of forms

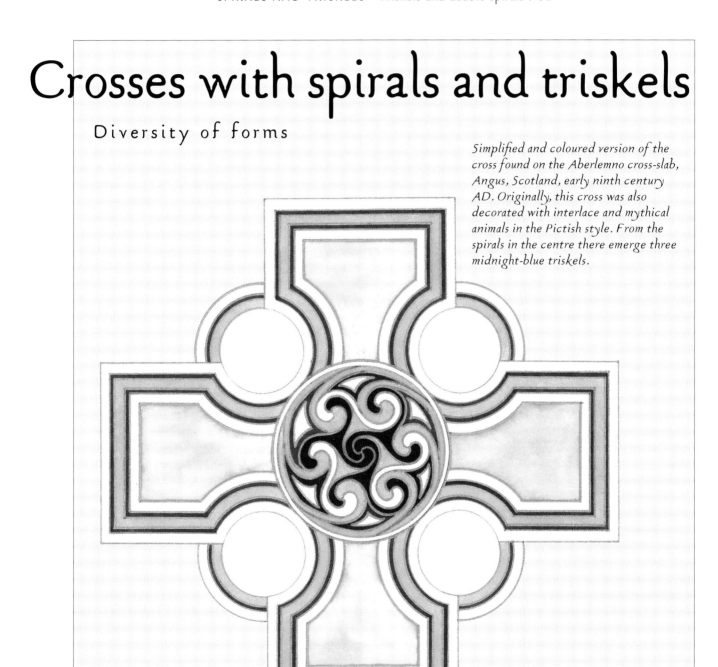

Simplified and coloured version of the cross found on the Aberlemno cross-slab, Angus, Scotland, early ninth century AD. Originally, this cross was also decorated with interlace and mythical animals in the Pictish style. From the spirals in the centre there emerge three midnight-blue triskels.

*Design inspired by the
North Cross at Ahenny,
County Tipperary, Ireland,
eighth to mid-ninth century AD.
The refined ornamentation of these
crosses is remarkable given the total
absence of remnants of religious
buildings in the vicinity.*

Detail of the Donore Disc,
County Meath, Ireland,
early eighth century AD.

Double spirals, triskels and foliage

Variations in colour

This double spiral appears on one of the miniature medallions incorporated into the complex network of spirals on a metal disc. The contrast between the colours reveals the refinement of the illustrator's technique.

Double spirals
with vegetal decoration

The evolution of a motif

Beginning in the fifth century BC, Celtic art developed a vegetal style that was new to the European artistic landscape between antiquity and the early Middle Ages. Celtic artisans showed great dexterity in the use of the compass, as with this 5 cm (2 in) double spiral.

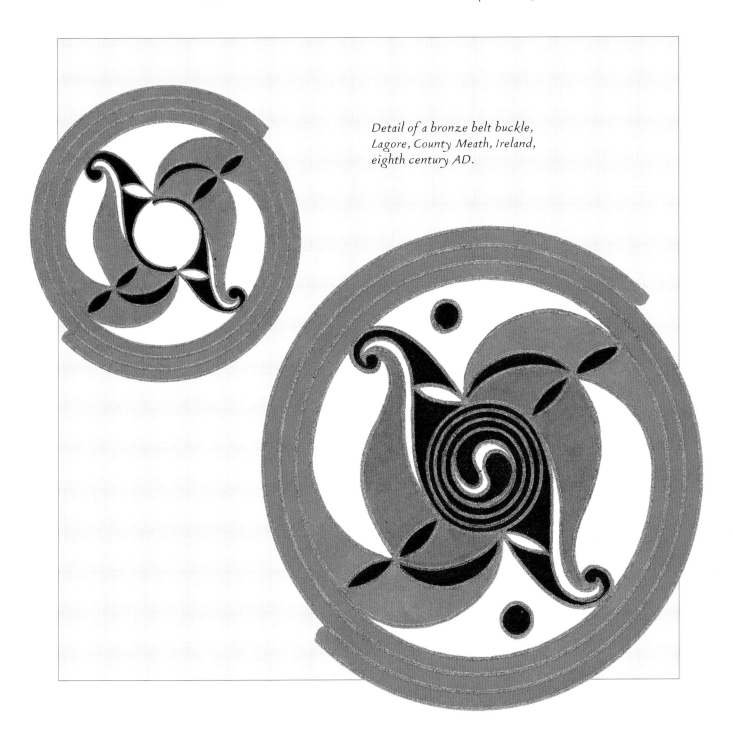

Detail of a bronze belt buckle, Lagore, County Meath, Ireland, eighth century AD.

Free spirals

In addition to the endless variations on the spiral and triskel,
organized for the most part around a central axis, some Celtic
artisans, particularly in pre-Christian Ireland and Britain, also
developed much freer spiral forms. From these new interpretations
arose original motifs, incorporated into decorative designs of
rare elegance. Their rediscovery in the nineteenth century
coincided with a search for new sources of inspiration
for the European decorative arts.

*Detail of a bronze scabbard, Lisnacroghera,
County Antrim, Northern Ireland, third century BC.*

*Decoration on a bronze
bracelet, Newnham
Croft, Cambridgeshire,
England, second
century BC.*

Emergence of the free spiral in friezes

Diversity of forms

Many civilizations count among their decorative repertoire the motif of waves in a frieze, a pattern that is particularly pleasing to the eye. By linking the wave with the free spiral shape, insular Celts perpetuated this decorative principle, bringing forth new spontaneity while avoiding the monotony of repetition.

Decoration on a bronze sword scabbard, Isleham, Cambridgeshire, England, late second or early first century BC.

Decoration on a metal plaque from Balmaclellan, Kirkcudbrightshire, Scotland, first century AD.

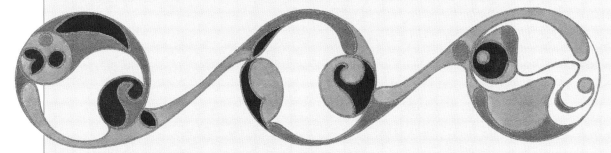

Decoration on a bronze sword scabbard, Deal, Kent, England, late second or early first century BC.

Mirror-back in tarnished bronze, Desborough, Northamptonshire, England, early first century AD.

Free spirals inside medallions

Diversity of forms

In the Celtic art of ancient Britain, a sharp-angled inflection or 'break' interrupts the curve of some spirals, thus giving birth to a type of hybrid leaf.

Detail of the decoration on a mirror-back, Holcombe, Devon, England, first century AD.

Decoration on the centre of a bronze horn, Saxthorpe, Norfolk, England, second or first century BC.

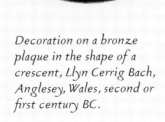

Decoration on a bronze plaque in the shape of a crescent, Llyn Cerrig Bach, Anglesey, Wales, second or first century BC.

Spirals and trumpets

Diversity of forms

Along with the 'broken' spiral and free composition of decorative designs, the Celtic art of ancient Britain is noted for the trumpet or fan motif.

Detail of a bronze mirror-back, England, first century BC to early first century AD.

Development of a shield boss, Llyn Cerrig Bach, Anglesey, Wales, second or first century BC.

Detail of a bronze mirror-back, England, late first century BC to early first century AD.

*Mirror-back, Nijmegen, the Netherlands, first century BC. This mirror,
found in the Netherlands, may have been imported from Britain in antiquity.*

Zoomorphic spirals

Diversity of forms

The British principle of inflected curves that end in small spirals is occasionally suggestive of a bird's head with a curved beak and large, hypnotic eyes.

Detail of the vegetal bird's head taken from the bronze pony cap at Torrs, Scotland, third century BC.

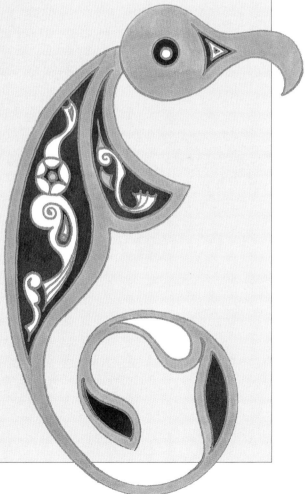

*Opposite page (right) and above: other vegetal birds engraved
on pieces of metal found in the Thames at Wandsworth, London,
late second or early first century BC.*

Book of Durrow, *folio 3v.*

Stylized horse head

The evolution of a motif

After centuries of Celtic creations, the Irish copyist monks perpetuated the features of an art of the imagination and of ambiguity: in the effusion of multiple spirals on a carpet page, an attentive observer can sometimes discern animal details, such as this miniature horse head (opposite).

interlace

Introduction p. 80

Interlace and trees of life p. 86

Single ribbon interlace p. 102

Interlace with animals p. 130

Introduction

Today, interlace is among the most popular Celtic motifs. Found on stone carvings, engraved jewellery or, more recently, on posters and album covers, the motif is a marker of Celtic identity. Paradoxically, it developed fairly late in the long history of Celtic art, namely during the Irish Golden Age. Probably inspired by the decorative patterns of neighbouring civilizations, the interlace motifs produced by the quills and chisels of Celtic artisans of the time underwent substantial refinement and growth, becoming one of the jewels in the crown of European graphic design.

Revival of the interlace motif during the early Middle Ages

Although a few early examples of motifs with interwoven lines appear in the continental European Celtic culture of antiquity, the interlace motif made its appearance during the Irish Golden Age beginning in the seventh century AD.

During that period, Europe was divided into three main cultural zones: the Byzantine Empire on one side of the Mediterranean basin, the Germanic kingdoms established further north in what had once been the Roman Empire, and the Celtic world, reduced to the 'Celtic fringe' we associate it with today (Ireland, Scotland, Wales, Cornwall and Armorican Brittany). Interlace patterns were also widespread in the artwork of the neighbours of the Celts during the early Middle Ages.

The Byzantine world perpetuated the decorative designs of ancient Greece. The torsade (decorative twisted braid or ribbon) of Middle Eastern origin evolved in archaic Greece into an interplay of lines drawn with a compass. In the classical period, the motif was multiplied on friezes in a guilloche (braided) pattern covering much longer surfaces, such as on the tympanum of the temple of Athena at Pergamon, built in the third century BC. On the elegant ceramics of the Hellenistic age, friezes of palmettes and other stylized vegetal motifs were then extended into ribbons that began to criss-cross or overlap in highly sophisticated ways.

The Roman Empire, heir to this repertoire of decorative form, carried on the interlace of vegetal motifs by incorporating vine tendrils and acanthus leaves on frescoes or *bas-reliefs* in patrician villas. On a larger scale, for public buildings in particular, abstract braids and interlace were multiplied to form friezes on Roman mosaics, appearing to acquire depth thanks to a subtle choice of *tesserae* (tiles) in nuanced shades.

After the decline of the western Roman Empire, Byzantium preserved the geometric interlace of these mosaics, adapting them to stone sculpture, to openwork panels on the chancel screens of the new Christian architecture and to capitals on columns within the basilicas. At the same time, richly ornate Bibles with friezes and crosses decorated with interlace, produced in the eastern Mediterranean regions, seem to have circulated amongst early Christian monasteries. During this time, in Egypt, Coptic tapestries also developed a repertoire of abstract interlace motifs, including elements of highly elaborate vines and trees of life.

In the early Middle Ages, interlace in the Mediterranean tradition appeared mainly in vegetal form, as well as in a more geometric pattern that we shall call the 'single ribbon'.

Around the time that the first signs of decline in the western Roman Empire were appearing, the Germanic tribes that threatened its borders to the north developed a singular range of highly stylized animal motifs, found for the most part on brooches and belt buckles. Undoubtedly inspired by classical Roman decorative models, these animal figures, already difficult to identify, began to break apart as the Germans advanced towards the south and west. In the late fifth century AD, limbs, heads and tails were juxtaposed in simple geometric forms.

It was in the sixth century AD, in southern Germany and in the new Lombard kingdoms of northern Italy, that the link was made between these motifs and the interlace of the Mediterranean tradition and an 'international Germanic style' emerged. In the kingdoms of northern and western Europe, fantastical animals took the form of highly stylized interlace patterns, such as on the belt buckle found in a Saxon tomb at Sutton Hoo (near Woodbridge, England), and on the jewellery found in numerous Merovingian troves.

Silver-plated side of the shrine of St Patrick's Bell (bronze, with inlay of silver, gold, crystal and glass), found in Armagh, Ireland, twelfth century. National Museum of Ireland, Dublin.

The magnificence and inventiveness of Celtic interlace

After the fifth century AD, the Irish Golden Age was born of the cultural syncretism between the new Christian faith and Irish society, still imprinted with Celtic traditions. This Golden Age would exert a discreet influence on part of what remained of the artistic world of western Europe. From the sixth century AD onwards, Irish monks moved across the continent, sometimes establishing monasteries in regions where Christianity lacked a foothold. The prestige of these monasteries was such that numerous pilgrims made their way to Ireland, in spite of the dangers of such voyages.

Until the tenth century AD, following these many forms of cultural exchange and under the protection of the monasteries, Irish artists produced sophisticated decorative motifs. These included highly complex interlace on Gospel books, furniture, liturgical vessels in gold and silver, and monumental crosses. The term 'Hiberno-Saxon' is often used to describe these works of art, since the relative contribution of each of the cultures — Celtic

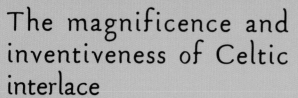

Gold brooch from Hunterston, early eighth century AD. National Museums of Scotland.

and Germanic — is so difficult to determine. Neither should the probable influence of the Mediterranean Christian world be forgotten.

Nevertheless, it is possible to identify some of the particularities of the single ribbon interlace produced by Irish artists and their disciples: the regular structure of the motif using diagonal lines; the use of central or axial symmetries; the rule of 'over-under' weaving; the principle of the endless ribbon; the elongated ribbon bent at its tip to fill certain empty corners of the composition; the alternation of colours along a single ribbon where the motif is painted; the link with the spiral motif developed by the Celts since antiquity, or with the labyrinth; and, of course, the fine detail of these motifs taken to a degree of complexity rarely equalled in the history of Western art.

The same types of single ribbon interlaces can be found on the pages of illuminated books, in filigree on jewellery or carved on monumental crosses from very diverse regions of the medieval Celtic world. Various theories as to the mode of transmission of these detailed interlace patterns have been put forward: a master artisan who possessed such a motif may have travelled throughout the Celtic world to teach artists and craftspeople the secrets of the design;

or else, by repeating the same basic knot patterns a number of artisans may have reached the same design solutions.

One can see that Celtic interlaced animals are treated more naturalistically than their Germanic cousins, while adapting and elongating their limbs according to the vagaries of the form. The Irish may thus have introduced to northern Europe the motif of the 'trees of life' populated by a variety of animals. Based on these distinctive features, one can identify as Celtic the interlace produced in Scotland, Wales, Cornwall or on the continent before the Carolingian era.

The Viking incursions into Celtic lands beginning in the eighth century AD, and the encounter between 'Hiberno-Saxon' interlace and Scandinavian variations on the late Germanic style, gave birth to a protean interlace in which it is often difficult to distinguish animal from vegetal patterns.

After the twelfth century, the interlace pattern would remain most prevalent in the decorative designs of Celtic peoples who were threatened or subjugated by the Anglo-Norman conquerors. A few objects still adorned with interlace survive, being of uncertain date but from somewhere between the thirteenth and sixteenth centuries, such as the famous harp of Brian Boru or the embossed leather satchel of the Book of Armagh, which recall the glorious past of an independent Ireland. Similarly, monumental crosses, brooches, swords and chests decorated with interlace attest to a Gaelic renewal in the Scottish Highlands and the Hebrides before the English put down the Jacobite Rebellion in the mid-eighteenth century.

After a gap of about a century, the mid-nineteenth century saw a rediscovery of traditional Celtic design — in its Irish and Scottish variants more precisely — by artists and archaeologists motivated by the need to affirm their identity and political views. This was the starting point for contemporary Celtic designs, of which interlace would be one of the leitmotifs.

The symbolic origins of interlace: threads, knots and weaving

To grasp the essence of a symbol as rich as interlace, we must reach back to the origins of the motif and civilization itself. The first interlace patterns — torsades and braids — appear to have derived from imitating the intertwined lines and forms associated with working with fibres and threads, such as rope-making, weaving, basketry or the production of nets. One might imagine that the first decorative braids appeared when ropes or baskets were accidentally imprinted on the damp clay of Neolithic pottery. The ancient origins of the interlace pattern would thus explain its universality, as it spread through the decorative repertoires of many civilizations.

Interlace is, by definition, a pattern formed by a thread or ribbon that criss-crosses in more or less complex twists. If the thread is continuous, and the two ends are pulled together, this often produces a knot. Let us now explore the symbolism of the knot and of the thread in traditional civilizations.

Amongst the most ancient known knot patterns are those of Isis in Egypt, representing eternity; of Solomon in the Jewish tradition, who was reputed to possess all the wisdom of the world; and of Heracles, with whom Alexander the Great identified. This last knot was thought to represent the way in which the hero tied the pelt of the Nemean lion. Alexander is also associated with the Gordian knot, which he sliced in two with his sword and thereby resolved, in a violent and unexpected manner, the hitherto insoluble problem of how to unloose it. In the Scandinavian tradition, there is the *valknut*, a magic knot consisting of three interlaced triangles, associated with the god Odin, who is sometimes known as the 'lord of the knot'. In the Far East, there is the mystical knot also known as the 'endless knot', which is one of the eight auspicious symbols in Buddhism: a symbol of the infinite wisdom of the Enlightened One and of the perfection expected of an accomplished Buddhist in whom wisdom and compassion should unite.

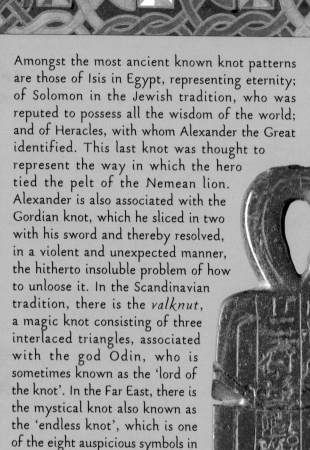

Amulet of Isis Knot on behalf of Said Sarbykhyna Iby, c. 1550-1295 BC.

Generally, the knot as a symbol bears within it the ambivalence of the principles of union and of deliverance. It obviously symbolizes the union of two beings, like the knots that are still used to tie together the clothing of a Hindu bride and groom in contemporary India, or the knots used to enact an unwritten agreement or contract in ancient societies. In ancient magical practices and popular medicine, knots were tied on parts of a sick person's body in order to preserve its vital forces, and knot-amulets were also worn as protection from the evil eye. Additionally, prayers were addressed to the gods for delivery from the evil bonds created by demons or enemy sorcerers.

This archetype of a magical bond unbound leads us to the symbol of the thread. Numerous traditions describe the work of implacable goddesses of fate: variously known as the Spinners, Parcae, Moirae, or Norns, they weave the fine thread of lives that intersect, thus creating the web of events in the universe. Eastern traditions often speak of veils, a reflection of the magic of the gods who are the masters of the bonds that a wise person must tear apart to free him- or herself from the illusion of creation. But these threads or bonds may also be seen from a more positive perspective: an ancient western tradition speaks of a *catena aurea* (golden chain) that is thought to link each element of creation directly to the divine. Along the same lines, in India, Brahmanic speculations give the name of *sûtrâtmâ* to the bond that connects each thing to its essence.

The symbolism of Celtic interlace as adopted in the Christian tradition

Let us return to the contemporary cultural context of medieval interlace in the Celtic tradition. During the Irish Golden Age, inspired by a great wave of Christian fervour, what could have been the symbolic value of these knots, threads and ribbons in an endless interlace?

The Old and New Testaments remind us of the ambivalence of the motif of knots, when they are tied together in the form of nets. Job, in his distress, declares: 'Know then God has put me in the wrong, and has closed his net around me' (Job 19:6). The Gospel of Luke more positively predicts the future mission of the apostles as 'fishers of men', symbolized by the miraculous catch of fish on the Lake of Gennesaret (Luke 5:11). Judaeo-Christian writings sometimes speak of God as a 'master of the bonds' who delivers the soul from the bonds of death. Christ, by rising from the dead, demonstrated the capacity of divine grace to free one from every earthly bond.

From the perspective of design, the best-known Christian symbol is that of the cross, which the Celts generously decorated with complex interlace and spiral motifs — notably on illuminated manuscripts — to the point that the symbol itself sometimes disappears in the profusion of designs. In this decorative exuberance it is interesting to note that ribbons crossing at right angles suggest additional small crosses, in a profound interplay of endless creation, revealing miniature crosses decorating much larger ones.

The triquetra, a triangle whose three sides are intertwined, may be read as a symbol of the Trinity, unless perhaps it is an allusion to the three knots on the rope belt worn by monks to recall their threefold vows of poverty, chastity and obedience. The interlaced vegetal motifs coming from a chalice appear to combine the tree of life, the tree of the knowledge of good and evil in Paradise, and the Tree of Jesse.

Interlaced quadrupeds, birds, fish-snakes and human beings in turn symbolize earth, air, water and fire (or spirit), respectively: as the four elements of creation they appear on the same carpet page of an illuminated book.

The Celtic principle of the endless ribbon could also suggest the notion of a bond and continuity between generations in the people of God, and between the past, present and future; thus representing the promise of eternal life to the believer. Finally, these infinite ribbons, like the paths of a labyrinth, may also have evoked, through a symbolic journey, the paths of spiritual initiation.

When the Celts of the early Middle Ages drew these admirable interlaced motifs, they did so, no doubt just like their ancestors in antiquity, from an awareness of the unity of the world, considering all of creation to be interconnected and to be connected to the same divine principle: the entire universe was seen as a giant and magnificent interlace.

Interlace
and trees of life

Interlaced vegetal tendrils are among the most captivating decorative motifs in the repertoire of Celtic forms. After the seventh century AD, the vegetal curves that were especially beloved of the pagan Celts were extended and criss-crossed over the parchment pages of illuminated Bibles and on monumental stone crosses. The Christian and Mediterranean models of vines populated by birds were transformed and adapted through contact with the flora and fauna of Ireland, the 'Emerald Isle'.

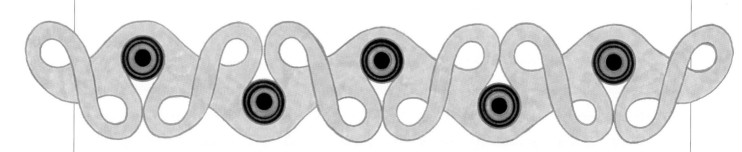

The Waldalgesheim Torc, Rhineland, Germany, fourth century BC.

The beginnings of interlace

Diversity of forms

Beginning in the fourth century BC, a new decorative style known as the 'Waldalgesheim style' made its appearance in Celtic art, characterized by undulating lines of curves and countercurves. On a few objects these lines overlap, thus creating the first interlace. However, it wasn't until the early Middle Ages that these motifs became standard features of the repertoire of Celtic forms.

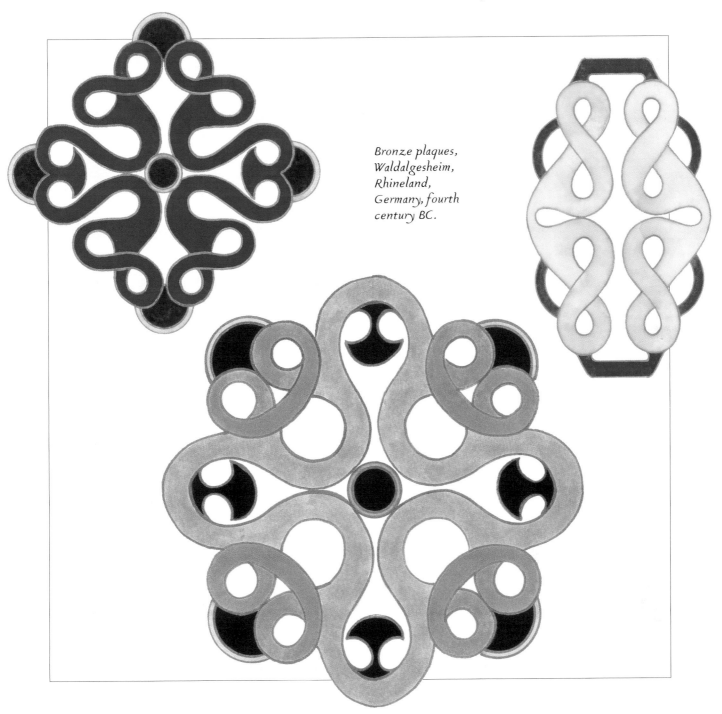

*Bronze plaques,
Waldalgesheim,
Rhineland,
Germany, fourth
century BC.*

Interlaced vines

Variations in colour and form

While it is sometimes difficult to identify the vegetal elements represented by Celtic artists, the vine branches here suggest the Christian (i.e. Mediterranean) motif of the vine. Leaving aside the foliage, or the animals with which Celtic trees of life are frequently interspersed, this motif is centred on the graphic line of the branches, linking spirals and interlace.

Motif on the Duleek North Cross, County Meath, Ireland, ninth century AD.

Motif from the Drumcliff High Cross, County Sligo, Ireland, ninth century AD. Here, engraved in stone, is the famous motif of the Old Testament tree of knowledge guarded by the serpent and surrounded by Adam and Eve. Note the originality of the double trunk, a part of which extends into the serpent, recalling the archaic symbol of the serpent wrapped around an axis. On a Sumerian vase, a double serpent slides along a pillar; it is associated with Ningizzida, god of medicine and 'lord of the Tree of Life'. This may be the prototype of the snake-entwined rod of the Greco-Roman god Asklepios/Aesculapius, the emblem of physicians to this day.

Chalices with rinceaux

Diversity of forms

The interlaced vegetal designs of Celtic art are often interpreted as vine motifs. Their rounded leaves, typically Irish in their treatment, are in fact more reminiscent of mistletoe, to which the Druids attributed the power of immortality. The lanceolate shape of the leaves of the Abercorn motif in turn suggests a Saxon influence.

From left to right: Book of Kells, *folio 114r.*

Book of Kells, *folio 114r.*

Stone fragment, Abercorn, Linlithgow, Scotland.

Book of Kells, *folio 8r.*

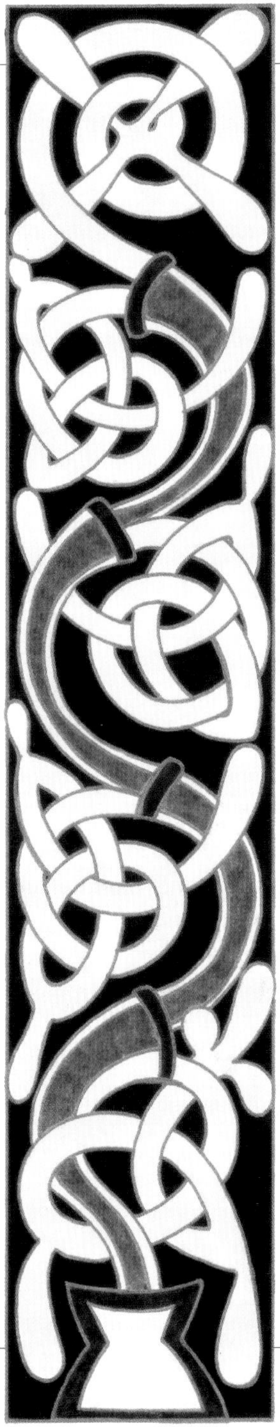

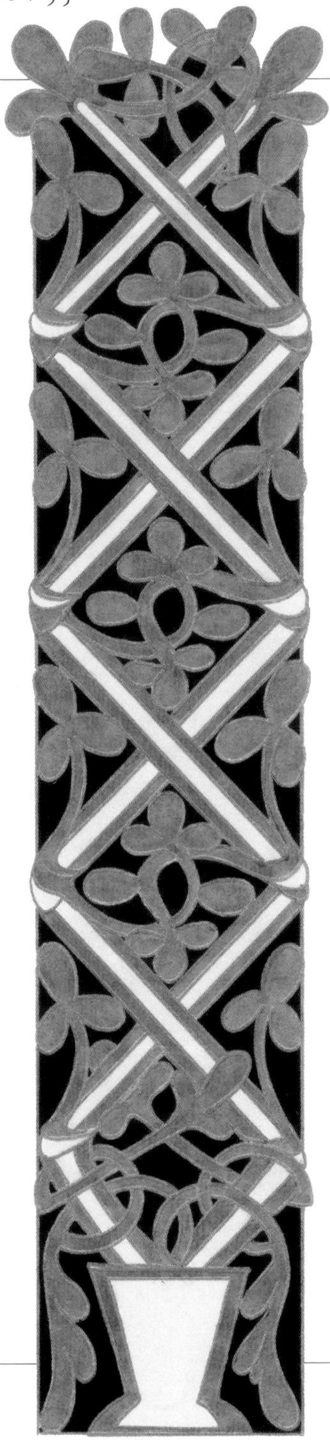

Designs inspired by the Bewcastle Pillar or Cross, Northumbria, early eighth century AD.

Double chalices with rinceaux

Variations in colour

In the Celtic iconography of Ireland and Britain there are numerous interlaced and exuberant vegetal motifs that appear to flow out of vases. The motif of the receptacle from which life springs forth is a universal symbol: the horn of plenty of the classical world, the *purna kumbha* in India, the *bao ping* vase of good fortune in Chinese Buddhism, and so on. In pre-Christian Celtic legends it appears in the form of a magic cauldron or a cauldron of immortality, and may lie at the origin of the Holy Grail, the object of the spiritual quest of the Knights of the Round Table.

Trees of life with double spiral

Diversity of forms

Book of Kells, *folio 202r. The profusion of vegetal interlace during the Irish Golden Age may be regarded as a visual interpretation of certain Judaeo-Christian texts that compare the newly baptized believer to a young plant which joins the ranks of the trees in the garden of the Church and will bear the fruit of spiritual abundance.*

Shrine of St Patrick's Bell, probably made in Armagh, late eleventh or early twelfth century. This motif is typical of the Scandinavian style we find in the interlace patterns produced in Ireland during the period. It could be interpreted as two dragons or as two interlaced vines.

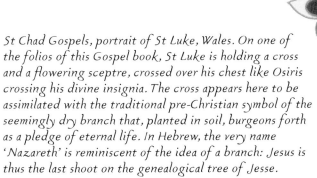

St Chad Gospels, portrait of St Luke, Wales. On one of the folios of this Gospel book, St Luke is holding a cross and a flowering sceptre, crossed over his chest like Osiris crossing his divine insignia. The cross appears here to be assimilated with the traditional pre-Christian symbol of the seemingly dry branch that, planted in soil, burgeons forth as a pledge of eternal life. In Hebrew, the very name 'Nazareth' is reminiscent of the idea of a branch: Jesus is thus the last shoot on the genealogical tree of Jesse.

Book of Kells, *folio 129v.*

Adaptation of a motif from the Book of Kells, *Chi-Ro (monogram) page, folio 34r.*

Book of Kells, *folio 129v.*

Book of Kells, *folio 285r.*

Chalices with flora and fauna

Diversity of forms

Here we have several versions of the rinceau coming out of a vase surrounded by birds, dogs or lions. According to some interpretations of the *Book of Kells,* quadrupeds represent the terrestrial world and birds the sky or the celestial world. It is the tree that links the two worlds to each other.

Adaptation made by the author of a panel on the Muiredach Cross, Monasterboice, County Louth, Ireland, ninth century AD.

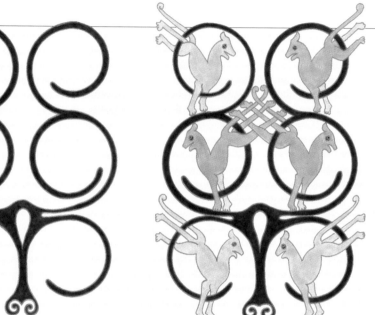

Trees of life and animals

The evolution of a motif

The Irish monumental crosses are renowned in the Celtic world for the symbolic richness of their ornamentation. According to certain authors, a number of them are veritable 'sermons in stone'. The Christian motif of the vine stock appears here as a tree of life, an allegory of the living Christ, populated by birds and quadrupeds that have been identified as strange squirrels. The legs of these animals provide the opportunity for a pattern of the interlace that was so beloved during the Irish Golden Age.

Single ribbon interlace

During the early Middle Ages, Byzantium, Ravenna and Lombardy preserved an ornamental repertoire that was spared the decline of the decorative arts after the fall of the Roman Empire. The Irish monks, indefatigable travellers who criss-crossed Europe, were inspired by the monumental stones, mosaics and textiles covered with abstract single ribbon interlace patterns they found on the continent, which we can still admire in the cultural centres of that period. Back in their home country, the monks reproduced and refined these motifs in the form of friezes and carpet pages covered in interlace, which constitute one of the glories of the Irish Golden Age.

Medallions with interlace

Variations in colour

The ribbons that escape from the central interlace are linked together by arcs. The traditional motif of interlace has thus been transformed, evolving and changing in accordance with the surface to be decorated. During the Irish Golden Age, we often find the same interlace patterns drawn in an illuminated book or carved on a monumental cross. Did the Celtic artisans reproduce their motifs from memory, or did they travel around with 'collections' of motifs?

Decoration on stone, Glamis,
Scotland.

Medallions with complex interlace

The evolution of a motif

The repetition of interlaced motifs on a frieze, or in the axial symmetry of a carpet page, can also be achieved by means of rotation within a circle. Although the Celts had possessed an unparalleled mastery of circular and spiral motifs since antiquity, only rarely did they use a compass to construct complex interlace designs. Several centuries later, artists such as Leonardo da Vinci and Albrecht Dürer would also produce circular interlace motifs, known as 'concatenations', for decorative purposes.

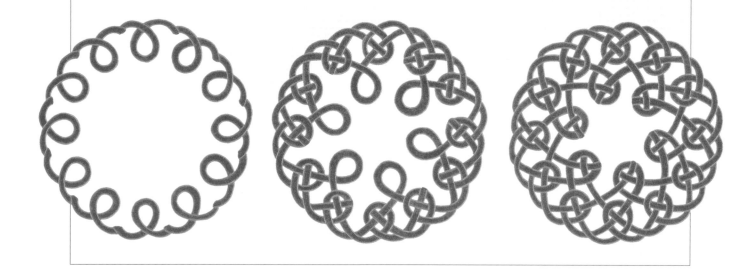

*Motif on a tombstone, Hilton of
Cadboll, Scotland, ninth century AD.*

Adaptation of the carpet page in the Book of Durrow, *folio 85v. This type of panel, linking interlace motifs enclosed within circular medallions, is found on mosaics and Lombardo-Byzantine openwork stone decoration from the seventh century AD. At the centre can be seen both a black 'cross pattée' adorned with green interlace and a diagonal cross with a vegetal theme, the dark-blue branches of which have a veined pattern.*

Frieze of medallions and carpet pages

Variations in motif and colour

Book of Durrow, *folio 3v. This angular development of a horizontal frieze in the* Book of Durrow *sums up the multiple sources of inspiration of Celtic interlace: alternating colours of Coptic or Syrian origin, circular medallions in the Lombardo-Byzantine style, and Celtic interlace hinting at shapes to be discovered. Here we can see a cross in the centre of each medallion.*

Friezes and medallions with pointed interlace

Diversity of forms

On this page the friezes and medallions of interlace are brought together: the flexibility of the ribbons is punctuated by inflections or 'points'. It is possible that these points are the means that Celtic artisans found to fill in the empty corners of certain decorative designs.

Lindisfarne Gospels, *folio 12r.*

Adaptation of the decoration on a stone slab, Inis Cealtra (Holy Island), County Clare, Ireland, ninth century AD.

Book of Kells, *folio 5r, and the Bealin Cross, Termonfechin, Clonmacnoise, Ireland.*

Ardagh Chalice, County Limerick, Ireland, early eighth century AD.

Motif carved in stone, St Vigeans, Perthshire, Scotland.

Adaptation of the decoration of the stone of Nigg, Scotland.

Book of Durrow, *folio 125v, and Kinnitty Cross (Castle Bernard), County Offaly, Ireland, ninth century AD.*

Crosses with 'pointed' interlace

It is difficult to determine with any degree of certainty the meaning of Celtic interlace. Certain motifs, often detached from their contexts, are at times arbitrarily referred to in pattern books or in jewellery as the friendship knot, the magical knot and so on. However, no reliable written source allows us to assign a definitive meaning to these Celtic knots.

Detail from the St John portrait page, Book of Kells, *folio 291r.*

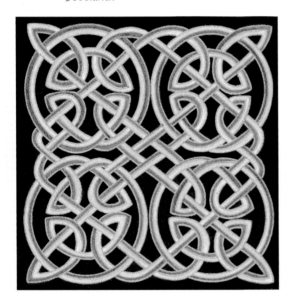

Adaptation of a motif carved on the Nigg Stone, Ross-shire, Scotland.

Motif carved on stones at Glamis, Angus and Collieburn, Sutherland, Scotland.

Multiple ribbon interlace

Diversity of forms

For these two circular motifs the endless interlaced ribbon has been cut into two or three ribbons of different colours in order to break the monotony of the single ribbon.

Crosses with interlace

Diversity of forms

Colour rendition of the cross on the Fahan Mura Slab, County Donegal, Ireland, seventh century AD. An inscription in Greek lettering on this early Irish cross reminds us of the erudition of the Irish Christian communities in the early Middle Ages.

Right: adaptation of a cross on a stone slab at Durrow Abbey, County Offaly, Ireland.

Opposite: an adaptation of a cross on a stone slab at Rossie Priory, Tayside, Scotland, eighth or ninth century AD. With its square ringed cross, this slab which features a complex interlace pattern and is also decorated with a wide variety of horseman and animal motifs (not shown), is very typical of carved Pictish stones.

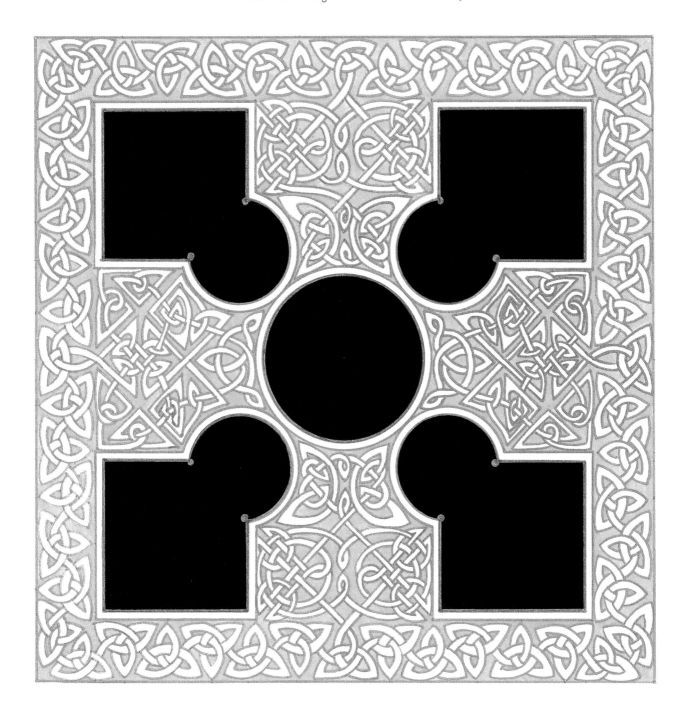

Friezes and carpet pages

Diversity of forms

The underlying principle of the Celtic interlace is the repetition of the same simple knot at regular intervals. Once the basic knot had been identified – in the nineteenth century, J.R. Allen distinguished twelve different ones – an infinite variety of compositions can be created by playing with the position of the knots and the links between them.

Book of Durrow, *folio 84v, and the high cross of Dysert O'Dea, Ireland, ninth century AD.*

Stone decoration, Dunfallandy, Scotland.

Book of Durrow, *folio 124v.*

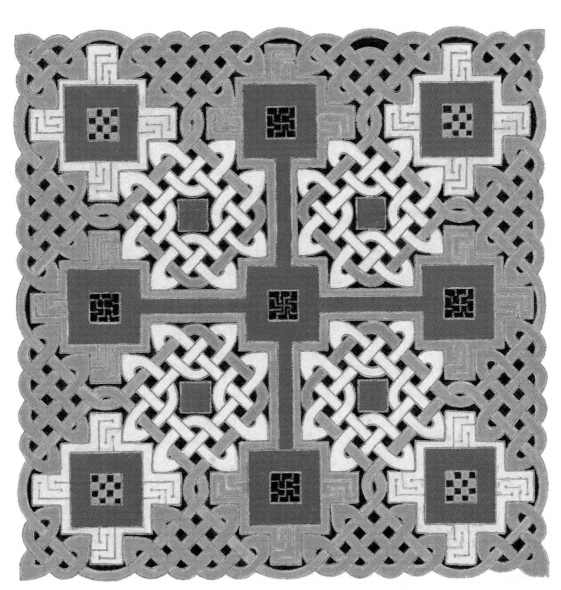

Adaptation of a carpet page from the Book of Durrow, *folio 1v.*

Interlace within a square

Variations in colour and form

The principle of alternating colours along the interlaced ribbon may have been inspired by Mediterranean motifs: early Christian Coptic and Syrian manuscripts already used this approach to avoid the monotony of endless ribbons.

*Adaptations of a
carpet page from
the* Book of Durrow,
folio 125v.

Carpet pages with interlace

Diversity of forms

Interlace designs are sometimes used to create labyrinths, probably drawing inspiration from the sumptuous metalwork with garnet cloisonné used in the Saxon and Germanic courts of the early Middle Ages. It is worth noting the repetition of cross motifs in these two adaptations of Irish designs. Are the interlace patterns constructed around the cross, or has the cross emerged from between the interlace designs? This interplay between shapes, which we can see at first glance, and others that emerge only upon closer examination, is typical of Celtic art throughout the ages.

Opposite:
Book of Durrow,
folio 248r.

High cross of
Dysert O'Dea,
County Clare,
Ireland, ninth
century AD.

Borders of interlace punctuated with squares

The evolution of a motif

Having left the monastery of St Comgall in Ireland and crossed the lands of the Franks with the famous missionary St Columban, St Gall settled as a hermit on the edge of Lake Constance in Switzerland in the early seventh century AD. The monastery that was founded on the site of his tomb was on the *Via Barbaresca*, a road used by Irish pilgrims en route towards Rome. Despite the distance, there is an unmistakable Irish influence in the decorative motifs of the books produced at that monastery in the early medieval period.

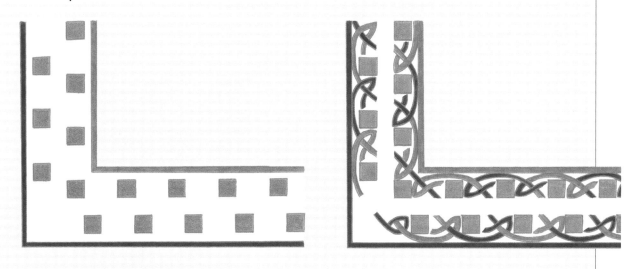

*Adaptation of a motif
from the St Gall Gospel book,
folio 209, Switzerland,
eighth century AD.*

Book of Kells,
folio 292r.

Friezes of complex interlace

The evolution of a motif

The *Book of Kells* never ceases to astonish with the fine detail of its decorative programme. Its interlace patterns are no larger than 2.5 cm (1 in). It is possible that the Irish copyists, having inherited a certain knowledge of geometry from their pagan ancestors, used optical instruments to achieve such a high degree of complexity.

Cross with interlace

The evolution of a motif

Motifs taken from the Dictionnaire des ornements *by Racinet, published in 1885, combined in the style of the carpet pages in Irish manuscripts. It was in the nineteenth century that the originality of the Celtic design repertoire within the vast panorama of medieval art began to be recognized. This dictionary of ornamentation appeared among numerous other collections of motifs at a time when Scottish and Irish artists were working on a revival of Celtic art that reflected increasingly assertive political movements.*

Interlace of triangular structure

Diversity of forms

By repeating a relatively simple triangular knot and a rotation at right angles, it becomes possible to obtain a square of regular interlace patterns.

Motif on a stone at Gask, Perthshire, Scotland.

Stone cross, Kilfenora, County Clare, Ireland, eleventh century AD.

Motif engraved in stone at the Church of St Peter at Britford, Wiltshire, England, ninth century AD.

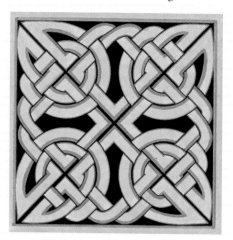

Opposite: Book of Kells, *folio 33r. In the thirteenth century, Giraldus Cambrensis described the* Book of Kells *as 'the work of angels', praising the minute detail in the carpet page decorations for which it was renowned. This complex motif is one of the four miniature interlace patterns that punctuate the margins of the 'cross of eight medallions'. Linking spirals, peltae (small shields) and strange animal heads, it is also distinguished by the original circular motion that seems to bring the lines of the motif to life.*

Interlace
with animals

The Germanic treasures of the early Middle Ages in the west
included jewellery covered with unidentifiable interlaced animals.
However, the Celts, who had a similar penchant for stylized
images from nature, opted for greater naturalism in their
treatment of animals, distinguishing snakes, bipeds and
quadrupeds. But although each animal is recognizable,
the limbs, ears, tongues and beaks are stretched
to suit the caprice of increasingly refined
interlace.

Interlaced dogs

Diversity of forms

Some art historians consider the interlace animals presented here to be dogs, inspired by the totemic animals of the Irish tribes of Ulster, who regarded them as faithful and tenacious. Other scholars, influenced by the Judaeo-Christian prejudice against dogs as impure animals, have preferred to see them as majestic lions. It is true that these animals sometimes sport flamboyant manes, particularly in the *Book of Kells*.

Book of Kells, *folio 29r*.

Adaptation of the decoration of the stone of Nigg, Scotland.

Book of Kells, *folio 29r. Three dogs with interlaced legs, suggesting a rotating movement.*
The original medallion is no larger than 4 cm (1 ½ in) in diameter.

Lindisfarne Gospels, *folio 95r. The Anglos and the Saxons who settled in Britain around the fifth century AD imported stylized interlaced animal motifs resembling dogs or dragons. The Celts, who were also fond of dogs, soon adopted those animal motifs.*

Lindisfarne Gospels, *folio 211r.*

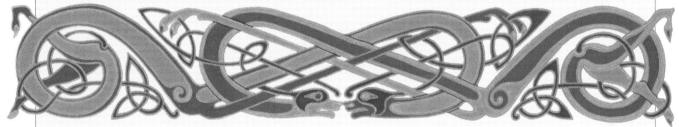

Lindisfarne Gospels, *folio 95r.*

Pairs of interlaced dogs

Diversity of forms

Interlaced animals in Celtic art may be distinguished from their Germanic ancestors by a return to a more naturalistic treatment of their morphology. Quadrupeds, represented in profile here, are generally portrayed either with one leg in front and one behind, or sometimes with all four legs. Their tails and ears are more freely extended into endless interlaced ribbons.

Interlaced serpents and birds

Diversity of forms

Detail of a carpet page from the Gospel of St John, Book of Kells, *folio 188r.*

In a Christian context, it may be surprising to see the representation of serpents – symbols of the devil – on Irish or Pictish monumental crosses or on illuminated crosses such as this one. One might be tempted to imagine that the snakes driven out of Ireland by St Patrick, as the legend has it, found refuge on the pages of the Book of Kells.

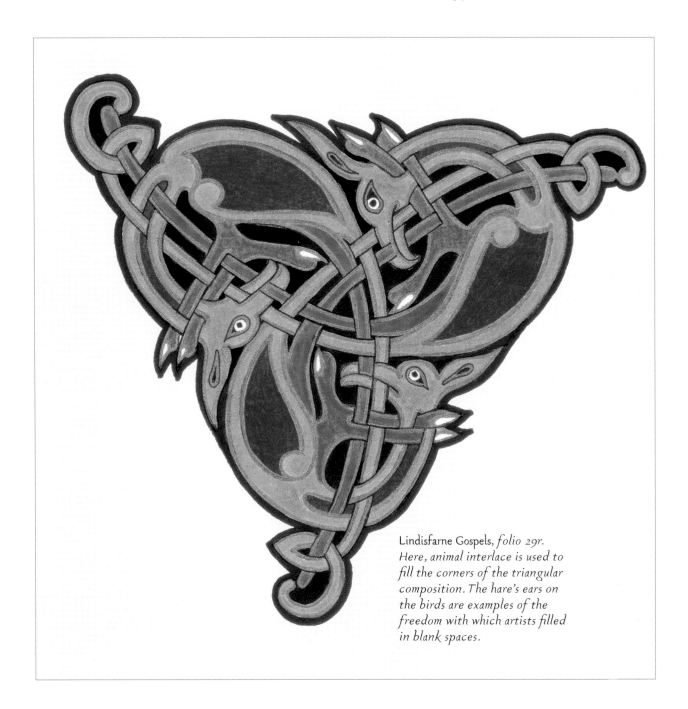

Lindisfarne Gospels, *folio 29r.
Here, animal interlace is used to
fill the corners of the triangular
composition. The hare's ears on
the birds are examples of the
freedom with which artists filled
in blank spaces.*

Book of Kells, *folio 29r.*

Medallions of interlaced serpents

Variations in colour

Interlace patterns had, since early antiquity, been serpentine in appearance. Here, the tips of the tails resemble eels and suggest fluidity and liveliness.

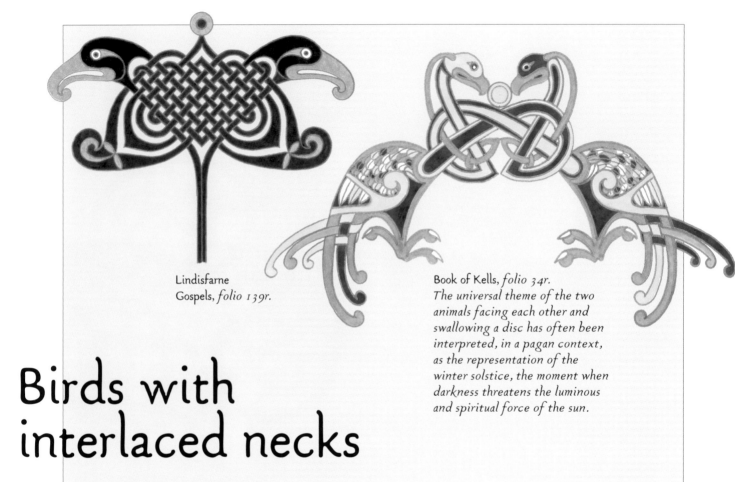

Lindisfarne
Gospels, *folio 139r.*

Book of Kells, *folio 34r.*
The universal theme of the two
animals facing each other and
swallowing a disc has often been
interpreted, in a pagan context,
as the representation of the
winter solstice, the moment when
darkness threatens the luminous
and spiritual force of the sun.

Birds with interlaced necks

Diversity of forms

In their quest for greater naturalism in the treatment of interlaced animals, the Irish of the early Middle Ages also developed the motif of the bird. Taking their cue from Christian symbolism, some art historians have thought these were eagles, the symbol of St John the Evangelist. But when we look at the elongated necks and legs, they seem more like waders.

Gospel book of Mac Regol,
folio 127, ninth century AD.

Book of Kells, folio 8r.

Zoomorphic letters with interlace

Variations in form and colour

During the early Middle Ages, Celtic artists achieved a perfect mastery of the interlace motif, to the point that they could play with them freely to create the bodies of amusing zoomorphic letters or use them as a filler across irregular surfaces.

Zoomorphic capital J, author's own design inspired by the Book of Kells.

Capital T with the body of a cat, Book of Kells, *folio 124r.*

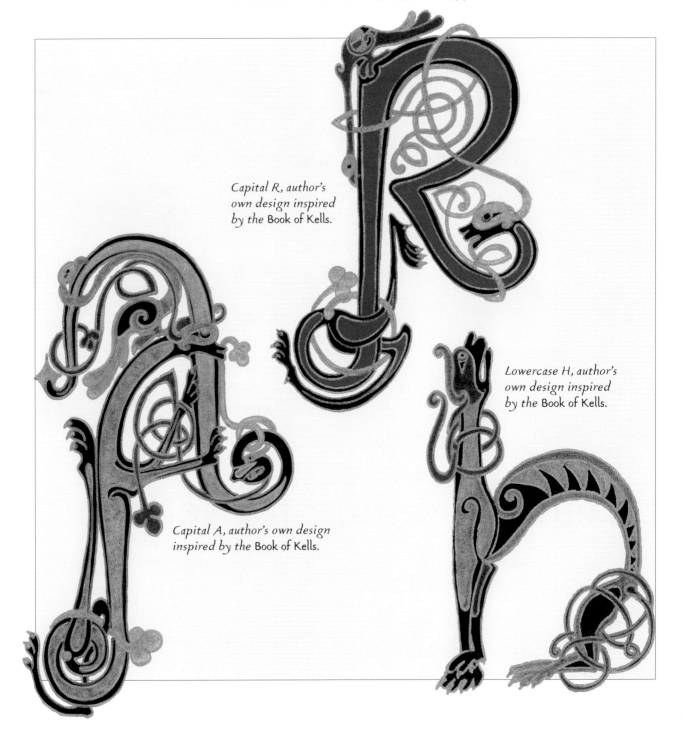

Capital R, author's own design inspired by the Book of Kells.

Lowercase H, author's own design inspired by the Book of Kells.

Capital A, author's own design inspired by the Book of Kells.

Capital W, author's own design.

Interlaced zoomorphic letters

Diversity of forms

Among the few illuminated books that survive from the Irish Golden Age, the *Book of Kells* is distinguished by the great variety of zoomorphic letters that playfully punctuate the occasionally austere lines of the four Gospels.

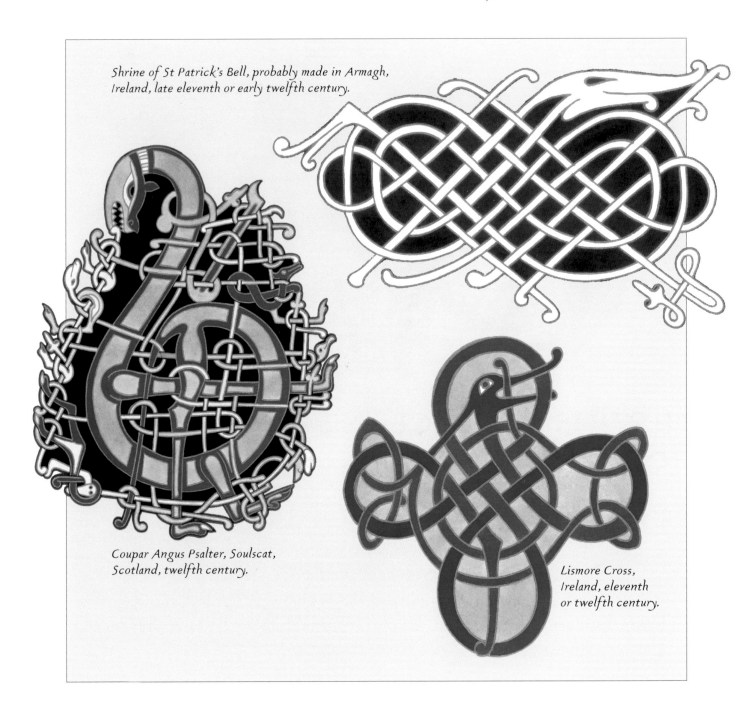

Shrine of St Patrick's Bell, probably made in Armagh, Ireland, late eleventh or early twelfth century.

Coupar Angus Psalter, Soulscat, Scotland, twelfth century.

Lismore Cross, Ireland, eleventh or twelfth century.

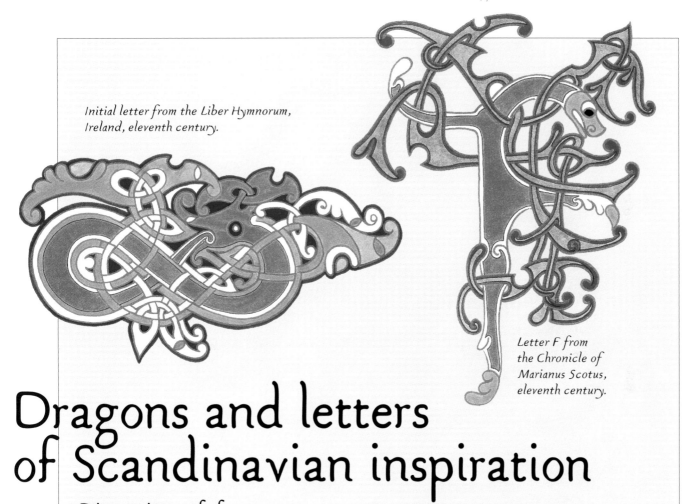

Initial letter from the Liber Hymnorum,
Ireland, eleventh century.

Letter F from
the Chronicle of
Marianus Scotus,
eleventh century.

Dragons and letters
of Scandinavian inspiration

Diversity of forms

Once the Vikings had established colonies on the shores of the Celtic world,
such as the one at Dublin, the Irish animal interlace patterns were transformed
under the influence of the Scandinavian style known as 'Urnes', recognizable
by its 'trumpet beaks', the burgeoning of plants from the limbs of dragons,
and the extreme complexity of interlace treatment.

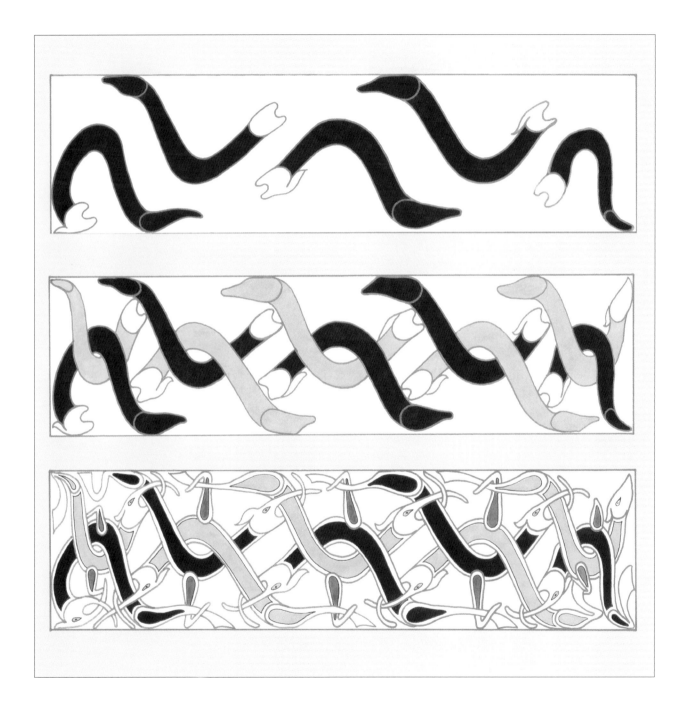

Frieze of interlaced dragons

The evolution of a motif

On this frieze, each animal grasps in its beak the serpent-shaped body of its neighbour. This posture recalls that of the interlaced animals of the pre-sixth century AD Germanic tradition, which are often difficult to identify. Some authors see in them the gryphon, a legendary animal with the body of a lion as the king of the beasts of the land, and the head and wings of an eagle as king of the creatures of the air. The red and yellow here, reproducing the colours of the original model, recall the amber and garnet that were used in metalwork of the early Middle Ages.

Book of Durrow, *folio 192v.*

LABYRINTHS

Introduction p. 152

Circular labyrinths p. 158

Medallions with labyrinths p. 160

Crosses with labyrinths p. 161

Carpet pages with labyrinths p. 166

Lozenge-shaped labyrinths p. 168

Diagonal labyrinths p. 170

Carpet-page elements p. 172

Introduction

One can tend to forget that the Celtic decorative repertoire also contains rectilinear and angular motifs, perhaps because subconsciously we associate these with other artistic traditions in which they are used more frequently. Nevertheless, chevrons, zigzags, lozenges, meanders or Greek keys and swastikas appear throughout the history of Celtic decorative art. These rectilinear motifs were especially prevalent during the formative Hallstatt period. They re-emerged in the early Middle Ages and the Irish Golden Age and developed into true labyrinths of particularly complex design on the pages of illuminated books and on monumental Celtic crosses.

Permanence of the labyrinth throughout the centuries

The European history of the rectilinear motif begins specifically with the exceptional mammoth ivory bracelet from Mezin, Ukraine, dated between 18,000 and 22,000 BC, depending on the source. What makes this piece exceptional is its coherent decorative system linking zigzags and meanders, which presupposes a degree of mastery of these geometric shapes that is unexpected for the period.

During the Neolithic era the invention of weaving and basket-making may explain the wider use of rectilinear decorative programmes. With these new techniques, playing on the colour of the fibres used in those arts, craftspeople readily created motifs using resilles (nets), lozenges, squares, chevrons, zigzags, steps, crosses, swastikas and meanders that, once combined, formed true labyrinths.

Beginning in the fifth millennium BC, between Anatolia and the shores of the Danube, these rectilinear motifs were also painted, moulded or incised in somewhat irregular patterns on seals, terracotta vases and figurines that probably represented mother goddesses. Later, during the second millennium BC, the geometric advances that enabled monumental architecture to be built in Mesopotamia and Egypt also made possible the creation of rectilinear ornamental patterns on the vast surfaces of temples or palaces.

In the ninth century BC, inspired by the geometrical rigour of these powerful neighbours, Greece developed a geometric style that systematized hand-painted rectilinear motifs inscribed within squares and regular bands covering very large ceramic pieces. Classical Greece later simplified these rectilinear patterns in the form of friezes of square meanders: thus was born the famous Greek key pattern, which would accompany, in bas relief, the majority of structures of classical inspiration over the subsequent centuries. The Romans, heirs to Greek culture, also used this motif frequently in their mosaics. Greek friezes adorned the floors of Roman buildings and, over time, they developed into veritable labyrinths; indeed, artists often used to depict, at the centre, the scene of the struggle between Theseus and the Minotaur.

After the fall of the Roman Empire, the Greek meander continued to be used in Byzantine design. Apparently, it is the origin of certain square motifs that decorate early Christian Bibles in the Greek East. In the new Germanic kingdoms established amid the ruins of the Roman Empire, in addition to chevron, zigzag and swastika patterns painted on rudimentary terracotta pieces, fine jewellery with stepped cloisonné patterns attests to a degree of refinement.

The hypnotic intricacy of the Celtic labyrinth

In the Celtic decorative repertoire, rectilinear motifs appeared principally in the formative phase of Celtic art and then during its final stage — the Irish Golden Age.

The very beginnings of Celtic civilization, from the eighth century BC, were marked by the repetition of rectilinear motifs on ceramics and metal objects. Examples of these include the pottery of Alb-Hegau, Germany, decorated in the style known as 'squares and fields', somewhat similar to Greek ceramics in the geometric style, alternating between empty spaces and surfaces covered in stamped zigzag or lozenge patterns. Also worthy of note is the tomb of a chief at Hochdorf, Germany, with its golden plaques and dagger adorned with the same highly refined decoration of repeated lozenges and zigzags, perhaps constituting an adaptation to metal of decorative motifs first developed for textiles.

With the advent of the Celtic art of the so-called 'classic style', in the fourth century BC, rectilinear motifs seem to have been eclipsed by the profusion of curved designs inspired by vegetal themes. Nevertheless, here and there we can still see a few decorative programmes that include swastikas, which share with the surrounding Celtic spirals the visual suggestion of rotational force. Examples of these include the patterns on a sword scabbard from Reziczer, Hungary, dating from the third century BC, and the Battersea Shield found in the Thames, London, and dating from the second century BC.

It was in the decoration of illuminated books from the seventh century AD that the Celts made their finest contribution to rectilinear motifs and created anew a series of true labyrinths. The books of Durrow, Kells and Lindisfarne reveal particularly complex decorative programmes masterfully combining spirals, interlace and other animal motifs in endless labyrinths. The regularity of the 'carpet pages', so-called because they are covered entirely with decoration, suggests that a minutely detailed preparatory grid must have been drawn on the page, on the basis of which the scribes could develop their maze-like lines.

Beyond the meticulousness of its construction, the specificity of the Celtic labyrinth of the early Middle Ages lies in its nearly consistently diagonal treatment, in the way the motif was twisted in order to enclose it within curved decorative bands, in the alternation of colours intended to break the monotony of the motif, and in the adaptation of motifs in stepped cloisonné work typical of their Saxon neighbours. Once the labyrinth had been mastered, the pattern was used during this period to decorate monumental crosses in Ireland, Scotland and Wales, and occasionally on items of jewellery or liturgical vessels.

Traditional labyrinths: protective devices and paths of initiation

Having observed how rectilinear decorative systems, some of which are incorrectly referred to as 'labyrinths', have come down through the centuries, let us now look at the traditional labyrinth form, which combines rectilinear and circular elements.

The traditional labyrinth (see illustration to the left) is drawn starting with the four corners of an imaginary square marked with four points, a central cross connecting the sides of the square, and four chevrons oriented parallel to the cross. Taking this underlying structure and linking the various elements with circular lines, the

Detail of a Roman mosaic of Theseus at Conimbriga, Coimbra, Portugal.

artist easily produces a set of seven arcs surrounding a single path giving access to the centre of the diagram.

Labyrinths that have been constructed in this manner can be found throughout the ancient world, from India via the shores of the White Sea to the Iberian Peninsula. These diagrams are, in some cases, carved in stone or even in the floor. A petroglyph (rock carving) with a traditional labyrinth, recently discovered in Chan do Lagoa, Galicia (Spain), dating from between 2500 and 1800 BC, is considered one of the oldest in the world. At Val Camonica, in the Italian Alps, labyrinths have been found carved on the walls of caves that probably go back to the Iron Age, and are surrounded by warrior or hunter figures armed with spears. Is this a representation of religious rites or the seat of an impregnable fortified city? The interpretation of these diagrams is still only speculative.

Certain myths describe inaccessible cities protected by labyrinths, such as the famous city of Troy. The Indian epic known as the '*Mahábhárata*' tells of the strategic military formation called the *chakra-vyuha*, 'which the gods themselves could not enter' and which is represented in Indian miniatures in the form of a labyrinth made up of rows of warriors. At Kurukshetra, on the very spot of that mythic battle, a temple dedicated to Shiva is decorated with labyrinths. This defensive motif recalls the *kolams* drawn by Indian women on the ground in front of their houses using rice powder.

Detail of a Roman mosaic showing Theseus slaying the Minotaur.

These traditional patterns, intended to guarantee the happiness of the household, often represent labyrinthine paths and swastikas which were supposed to imprison demons (since it was believed that they could only move in straight lines), or to prevent them from entering the house.

Likewise in India, tantric symbols including traditional labyrinth motifs were used as talismans by women in childbirth. The association of the labyrinth and birth recalls the rectilinear decorations using chevrons, meanders and lozenges of Neolithic figurines of mother goddesses, as mentioned above. These decorations may be a symbolic representation of the flow of fertile waters. The structure of the labyrinth thus offers protection at the critical passage from virtuality to the physical manifestation that is birth.

In Greco-Roman tradition, the theme of the maze also evokes the famous legend of the Minotaur. King Minos of Crete had asked the architect Daedalus to build a complex structure in which he could lock up the Minotaur, fruit of the union of his wife Pasiphae and a bull sent by Zeus. Every year, the Athenian subjects of King Minos sent a contingent of young men and women to be fed to the monster. At length, Prince Theseus undertook to enter the labyrinth, succeeded in slaying the Minotaur and made his way back out of the maze thanks to the thread given him by Ariadne. Symbolically, the Minoan labyrinth may be taken to refer to the meanderings of the human soul through which a hero, an initiate or a perfected human being emerges more mature, after having slain his inner demons and returned to the real world guided by the thread of a clear conscience.

The Celtic labyrinth: borrowed or born of Celtic legend?

The pre-Christian Celts knew how to draw traditional labyrinths, as can be seen from a Bronze Age carving on the stone known as the 'Hollywood stone' because it was found in 1908 near Hollywood, County Wicklow, Ireland. Like most ancient symbols, attempts to interpret them yield more questions than answers. However, when one reads the Celtic legends one finds some surprising connections that prompt speculation, for example between a petroglyph in Val Camonica representing a horned figure with a serpent belt that wraps itself around him in the form of a labyrinth, and the Irish legend of Conall Cernach, who journeyed to the Alps to confront the serpent guarding a fort in which the herd of sacred cattle belonging to the goddess Boand was kept imprisoned.

Although the Christian Celts, whether Irish, Welsh or Scottish, rarely used the labyrinth motif in its traditional form, they nevertheless developed highly complex maze patterns on stone and parchment. It is not certain whether they attributed symbolic value to these carpet pages covered in meanders. Perhaps they followed the paths of these labyrinths with their eyes and imagined a symbolic pilgrimage to the heavenly Jerusalem, as believers would later ritually walk along the mazes that decorated the paving stones of certain cathedrals, such as Chartres.

Whatever their interpretation, the Celtic labyrinth never ceases to fascinate us, as we mentally follow its endlessly meandering path. The same principle is at work in the visual development of the spirals and interlace produced by Celtic artists: if their lines are disorienting, causing us to lose for a moment all sense of time and place, it is in order to transport us symbolically to another dimension — one that is conducive to meditation and contemplation.

Circular labyrinths

Diversity of forms

The motifs of traditional labyrinths have for millennia been circular in shape, as seen on the walls of several European caves and on Minoan coins. Here we have two rare examples of a labyrinth with a circular structure made by Irish monastic scribes, who generally preferred to treat this motif in square structures or on carpet pages.

Adaptation of a disc in the Book of Mac Durnan, Ireland, ninth century AD.

Adaptation of a disc in the Book of Kells, folio 32v.

Decoration on a stone slab at Pen Arthur, Wales, early Middle Ages.

Medallions with labyrinths

Diversity of forms

Central medallion on the West Cross in a field in Kilfenora, County Clare, Ireland, twelfth century.

Decoration on a stone slab at Clonmacnoise, County Offaly, Ireland.

Detail of a stone slab at Inchagoil, County Galway, Ireland, reminiscent of a Chinese ideogram.

Crosses with labyrinths

Detail of the carpet page of the four evangelists, Book of Kells, folio 27v. Another example of the extremely fine detail of the Irish scribes, this cross is no larger than 8 cm (3 in). Rivalry between the different monasteries during the Irish Golden Age seems to have given rise to a form of artistic competition among copyists, and may account for some of these marvels of design.

Crosses with labyrinths

Diversity of forms

Enclosed within squares, certain Celtic labyrinth motifs appear to be developments of the symbol of the cross.

Detail from the Lindisfarne Gospels, *folio 211r.*

Detail from the Book of Mac Durnan, *folio 4v, Ireland, ninth century AD.*

Detail of the West Cross in a field in
Kilfenora, County Clare, Ireland, twelfth
century. This motif is also carved on
the cross of Houelt (see page 164),
in Wales, suggesting that decorative
motifs were disseminated throughout
the Celtic world.

*Detail on the Bealin Cross, County Westmeath,
Ireland, c. 800 AD.*

Detail of the decoration on the throne
of the Virgin, Book of Kells, folio 7v. This
composition recalls the ornamentation of
certain Byzantine reliquaries that may have
circulated throughout the Christian
world early in the Middle Ages.

Crosses with labyrinths

Diversity of forms

Reconstruction and colour rendition by the author of the stone cross of Houelt at Llantwit Major, South Glamorgan, Wales, ninth century AD. An inscription states that King Houelt had this monument erected as a memorial for the salvation of his father Res in AD 886. Of all the carved stones and monumental crosses of the Celtic Christian world, the 'disc-headed' stone slabs of Wales stand out with their refined decoration.

Opposite: adaptation of a cross carved on a stone slab at Tullylease, Monastery of St Berichter (or Berchert), County Cork, Ireland, eighth century AD.

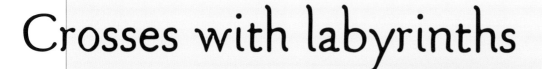

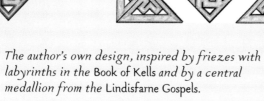

The author's own design, inspired by friezes with labyrinths in the Book of Kells *and by a central medallion from the* Lindisfarne Gospels.

Carpet pages with labyrinths

The evolution of a motif

The labyrinth motif, with its perpendicular lines, may draw its inspiration from weaving. Some Celtic illuminated manuscript pages, covered entirely with decorative motifs, are known as carpet pages. It is conceivable that Celtic textile artists may have produced masterpieces of embroidery, carpets or tapestries in this style, which has long since disappeared.

Author's own designs, inspired by the labyrinth motifs of the Lindisfarne Gospels, folio 210v.

Lozenge-shaped labyrinths

Variations in colour

Here, a detail taken from a labyrinth that covers a carpet page, treated as a motif in itself. The variations in colour suggest a similarity with the decorative patterns of ancient Chinese bronzes and Central American architectural motifs, among others.

The author's own design, based on a central motif taken from the Book of Kells.

Diagonal labyrinths

Diversity of forms

One of the particularities of the labyrinths that decorate illuminated Celtic manuscripts is their almost systematically diagonal format.

Central motif taken from the Book of Kells and a border adapted from a motif in the Lindisfarne Gospels.

Carpet-page elements

Variations in colour

Certain motifs of the early Middle Ages, which have been extracted from their often highly decorative programmes, may appear quite archaic to an observer today but are, in fact, strangely modern. Here, a labyrinth of Irish origin takes on the appearance of a microprocessor.

The author's own design, inspired by the Book of Kells.

bestiary

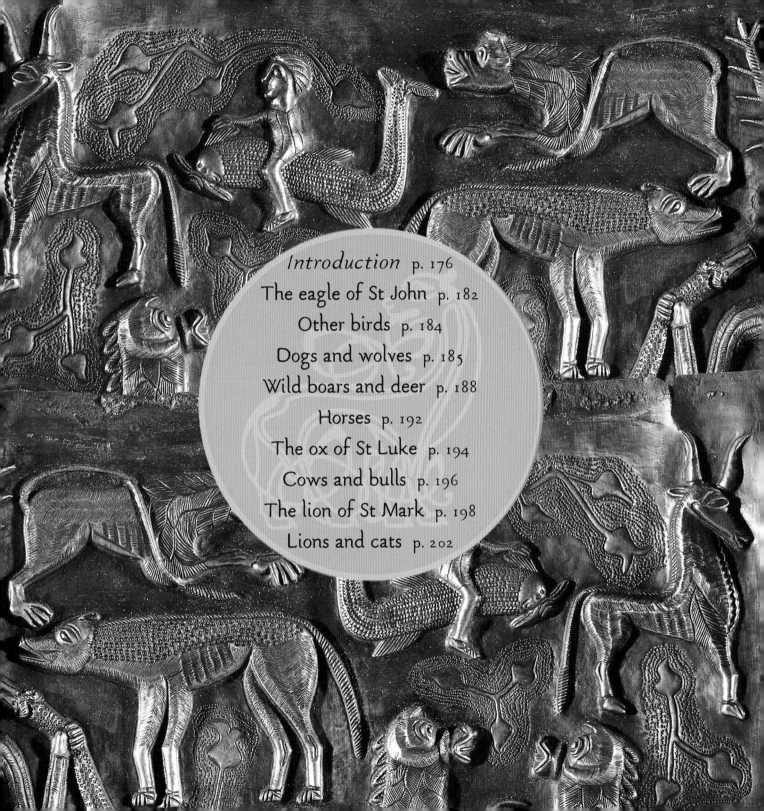

Introduction p. 176

The eagle of St John p. 182

Other birds p. 184

Dogs and wolves p. 185

Wild boars and deer p. 188

Horses p. 192

The ox of St Luke p. 194

Cows and bulls p. 196

The lion of St Mark p. 198

Lions and cats p. 202

Introduction

Celtic culture, like many traditional cultures, developed in close harmony with nature. Accordingly, animals were among the favourite subjects of Celtic artists. From the first representations of beasts, albeit in somewhat schematic form, in the Hallstatt period of the eighth century BC, to the highly stylized figures of the early Middle Ages, the Celtic bestiary of course experienced a great variety of styles. A feature common to them all, however, is the great freedom taken by the artists, who were prepared to distort the body of the animal into unexpected decorative patterns and, starting out with other abstract motifs, to suggest heads or entire bodies of imaginary animals.

Animals in the Celtic world

The Celts were able to dominate the northern European world in ancient times thanks to two discoveries: iron and the use of horses. Armed with their steel swords and mounted on small, speedy horses, the first Celtic horsemen of the eighth century BC had no difficulty prevailing over the comparatively peaceable early peoples of Europe. The horse, as in most Indo-European civilizations, was the principal attribute of this new military aristocracy, of which the Knights of the Round Table were the direct heirs. The dog seems to have been one of the Celtic

Relief on the Gundestrup Cauldron (silver-plated copper, partially gilded) found in a peat bog near Gundestrup, Jutland, first century AD. National Museum of Copenhagen.

warrior's most faithful companions; Old Irish texts even mention certain particularly laudable fighting dogs.

Not all Celts were horsemen, however. Animal husbandry occupied a large proportion of the population. The bones of cows, sheep, pigs and poultry found in many archaeological sites attest to the importance of those animals to the Celtic economy. Wealth was measured in heads of livestock, and cattle-rustling, a common occupation of certain 'Celtic cowboys', could provoke full-scale wars.

Hunting and fishing were also resources of the Celtic economy. The Celtic landscape consisted of a series of islands of cultivated land surrounded by an ocean of ancient forests. There is some uncertainty about the consumption of large game such as wild boar, deer, wolves and bears. Based on recent studies by historians, these animals, no doubt considered sacred by the Druids, may have been subject to a taboo prohibiting their consumption. It may be that roast boar never in fact graced the table during the banquets of Asterix.

Unusual Celtic animal representations

The first animal representations during the period of the powerful rulers of Hallstatt in central Europe, around the eighth century BC, consisted of small deer, aquatic birds and horses in the form of votive figurines or decorations on ritual objects. We can also see mythological animals, inherited most likely from the Mediterranean or Middle Eastern cultural worlds, such as the winged horse of the torc and the gorgon on the immense krater of the Princess of Vix (see page 16). In the fourth century BC, Celtic artists began to draw their inspiration in part from the repertoire of forms of neighbouring cultures: Etruscans, Greeks and Phoenicians.

After the fourth century BC, at a time when they were expanding rapidly throughout northern Europe, the Celts developed a characteristic style of highly exuberant vegetal, animal and human forms. This style, known as the 'La Tène', made a clear break from classical Greek and Roman figurative art. On bracelets, for example, horned

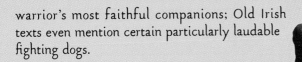

Bronze fibula in the shape of a dragon, in Romano-Celtic style, first century AD. Private collection.

The incursion of the Romans into this universe of Celtic forms led, after the conquest of Gaul by Julius Caesar, to the development of a Gallo-Roman art form that linked, sometimes awkwardly, the stylized animals of the Celts with the figurative canons of classical art. That fusion brought to an end this chapter in the history of Celtic art in continental Europe.

Celtic art continued its stylization of living beings in Ireland and Britain, away from mainland Europe. The Roman conquest was shorter and less influential in these regions than elsewhere, and powerful local elites with well-established tastes enabled an insular Celtic art to flourish that is recognisable by its great refinement. The skilful use of the compass led to the appearance of new figures of enigmatic birds and cats that seem to play at riddles with the viewer.

Around the fifth century AD, the conversion of the last of the Celtic peoples to Christianity in Britain and Ireland gave rise to a flourishing Celtic Golden Age. Animals now came to adorn reliquaries, the extraordinary illuminated books of Kells, Durrow and Lindisfarne, and the famous Celtic crosses. The animals that symbolized the evangelists were recurrent motifs — we will return to these below — and the artistic representations of animals in this period are characterized mainly by the elongation of their bodies in order to include them within a highly complex system of interlace patterns inspired, no doubt, by contemporary Saxon objects. Contacts (peaceful or otherwise) with Viking culture continued this penchant for elongation in a style some historians refer to as 'Hiberno-Viking art'.

Bronze statuette of a horse with a human head. Celtic art, second half of the fifth century BC. Saarland, Germany.

serpents appear among vegetal rinceaux, while on sword scabbards deer gambol on curving paths and bizarre dragons seem to come face to face. Alongside votive figurines that were by now 'Celticized', coins became the medium for completely original stylized representations, with horses and human faces breaking up into a juxtaposition of abstract shapes.

In the middle of the twelfth century the conquest of the last Celtic territories by the Anglo-Normans brought to an end this original Celtic artistry. It wasn't until the revival of Celtic art in the nineteenth century that these stylized forms of animal representation made their reappearance.

A pagan animal symbolism

Among domestic animals, the horse occupies a privileged position. Important Hallstatt chiefs were buried with their warhorses, and the sumptuous elegance of the harnesses found in Britain attests to the high esteem in which these animals were held, on a par with the honour accorded to certain human beings. In the Ulster Cycle, the Grey of Macha and the Black of Saingliu, the magical horses of the hero Cú Chulainn, are endowed with human intelligence. Celtic coins seem to share with other Indo-European mythologies, notably the Greek and Indian, the figure of the warhorse pulling the chariot of the sun, or the chariot that leads souls to the afterlife. Finally, we should not forget one of the few goddesses of Gaulish origin accepted into the Roman pantheon: the mare goddess Epona, whose protection Roman legionaries soon began to invoke. This goddess is thought to be at the origin of the legendary Welsh figure Rhiannon or Pryddein, of whose name Britannia may be a distorted version.

Like the horse, the dog, despite the negative image attributed to it by the clergy, had long been valued by the Celts. Dogs also appear frequently in their myths as guardians of the gates of heaven, or as heralds announcing the arrival of one of its inhabitants. This symbolism is probably a legacy of ancient Indo-European archetypes. The name Cú Chulainn, the Irish national hero, means 'dog of Culainn'. At the tender age of five he struck down the mastiff of a noble house and, by way of compensation, was ordered to take the animal's place for a period of time. The Irish warrior class deliberately sought this association with the dog, which symbolized bravery and combativeness. Even a well-known patronymic such as O'Connor derives from the Gaelic root *cu* or *co*, meaning 'dog'.

The antlered Celtic god Cernunnos, holding a torc in one hand and a ram-horned serpent in the other, surrounded by deer and cats.

The cow and the bull were in turn considered incarnations of abundance. The vigour of the bull, protector of the herd, symbolized strength and the royal power that guaranteed the prosperity of the nation. The bull gods of Mesopotamia and Crete were the first examples of these archetypal protectors. An Irish legend, the *Cattle Raid of Cooley* (also known as the *Táin*), is an allegory of the race for power and wealth. Maeve (Medb), the queen of Connaught, has as many heads of cattle as the king. To increase her power, she has the 'Brown Bull of Cooley' stolen from Ulster, unleashing a formidable war. There are also certain Celtic figures that represent a strange-looking bovine: the *taurus trigaranus*. The three horns of this bull may be associated with the three phases of the moon.

Among the wild animals, the boar long enjoyed the respect of the Celtic warrior class, since it is one of the few animals that will fight back against its aggressors. Springing with lightning speed from its wallow, it was spontaneously associated with the thunder of Taranis, the Celtic god of the heavens. The male boar, a solitary forest dweller, was also apparently the emblem of the priestly class. The sow, surrounded by her many offspring, may have symbolized the Druid surrounded by his disciples. A Welsh legend tells of the hunt for the giant magical boar Twrch Trwyth, guardian of the treasure that would enable Kulwch, the nephew of Arthur, to marry the beautiful Olwein.

The deer, a more peaceable creature, was nevertheless equally fascinating to the Celts due to its mysterious antlers, the life of which seem to follow the cycle of seasons and plants. This life force, endlessly reborn, is at the origin of the horned god identified as Cernunnos on certain Gallo-Roman inscriptions. These pagan images may have influenced the representation of the devil in Christian iconography as a horned figure. Ironically, one of the most famous Celtic saints, St Patrick, was said to have changed into a deer to escape his attackers, thus imitating several figures in Celtic lore who also had a predilection for the form of a deer for their metamorphoses.

As for the bear, it was a symbol of royalty for the Celts, connected to the notion of the pole or axis safeguarding the stability of the universe. The Celtic root *arto* is at the origin of the name of the renowned Arthur, as well as of the Welsh name for the constellation *Ursa major* (the Big Dipper), *cerbyd Arthur*, or 'Arthur's chariot'.

Celtic mythology is filled with episodes in which birds influence human destiny, including the magical and healing birds of Rhiannon, the adulterous woman Blodeuedd transformed into an owl, and the warlike fury of the crow goddess Bodb. Pride of place is given to swans, the incarnation of exceptional persons, often represented as couples linked to each other by a chain of red gold. In Britain today, these majestic birds are protected and considered the property of the queen.

Finally, contrary to popular belief, the dragon appears only very late in the Celtic bestiary. In Welsh legends and Arthurian tales, two dragons regularly engage in combat, causing much damage along the way. We can recognize in these stories the theme of two dragons guarding the tree of life or the spring of youth, which dates back thousands of years.

The animal as a religious symbol

It would be impossible to end this chapter on animal symbolism without speaking of the symbols of the evangelists, even though their representations are not Celtic in origin. Perhaps inspired by the vision of Ezekiel, the Apocalypse of St John describes Christ in majesty on a throne surrounded by four living creatures, each with six wings and covered with eyes: the lion, the ox, the man and the eagle – thus constituting the tetramorph. These creatures would later become the symbols of St Mark, St Luke, St Matthew and St John respectively, allegories of the Christian message that medieval artists and scribes, particularly the Irish, would develop in great abundance.

Faced with this profusion of symbols, it would seem futile to try to identify what is distinctive about the sacred bestiary of the Celts. As in any traditional civilization, in which no distinction is made between the sacred and the profane, artists certainly were less intent on representing the particularities of the animals in their midst than on capturing the essence of the animal archetypes that populated their symbolic world. Thus Celtic art, with its stylized bestiary, leads us into a universe where reality and the imaginary are but one.

Introductory page to the Gospel of St Matthew representing the winged symbols of the four evangelists, from the Book of Kells, *ninth century AD. Trinity College, Dublin.*

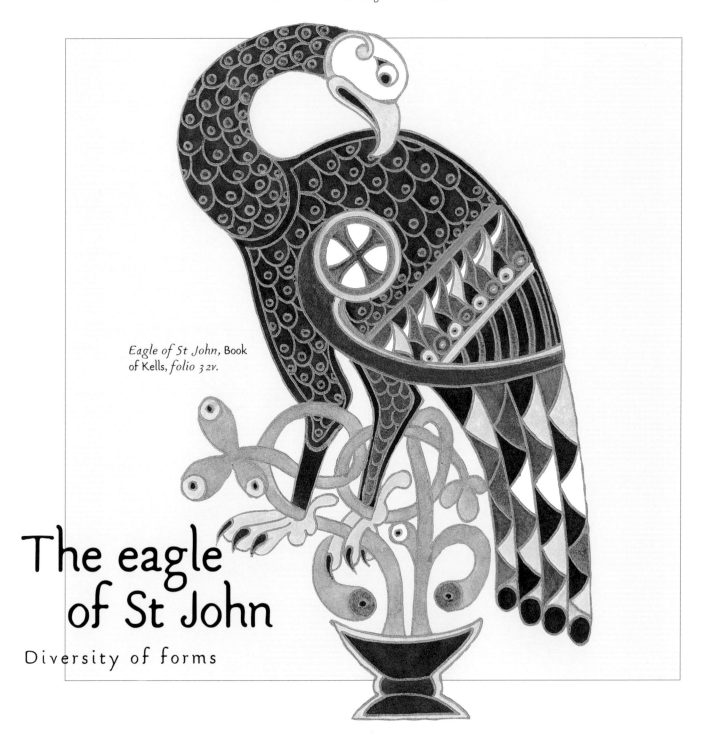

Eagle of St John, Book of Kells, *folio 32v.*

The eagle of St John

Diversity of forms

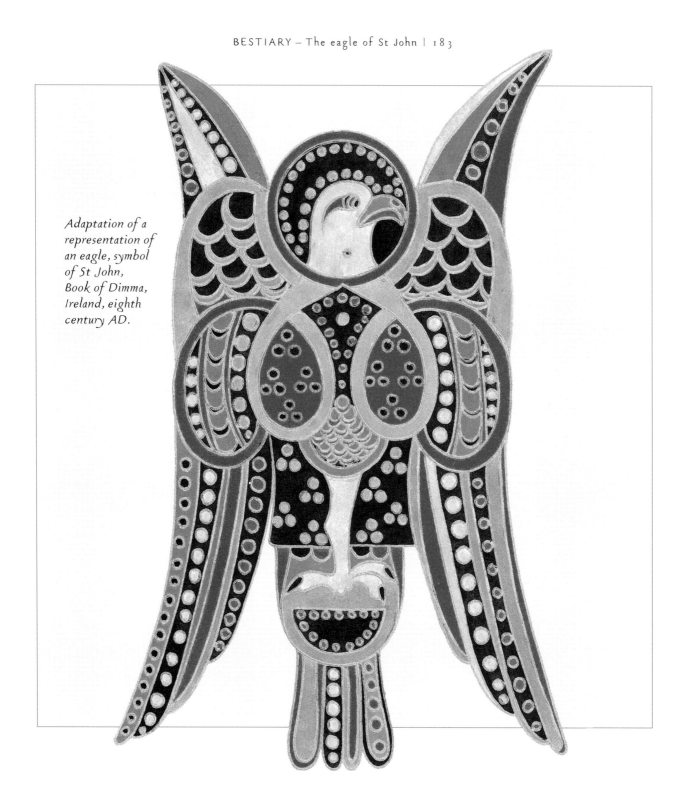

Adaptation of a representation of an eagle, symbol of St John, Book of Dimma, Ireland, eighth century AD.

Other birds

Eagle, Book of Kells, *folio 31or. The pages of the* Book of Kells *include not only the eagle, symbol of St John, but a large number of other flying creatures that are sometimes difficult to identify.*

Goose or dove, Book of Kells, *folio 200r.*

A peacock, Book of Kells, *folio 277r. Well before the cross, the peacock or the fish was used to represent Christ. The flesh of the peacock was believed to be incorruptible: an allegory of the eternal life promised to all Christians.*

Dogs and wolves
Diversity of forms

Pouncing dog,
Book of Kells, *folio 19v. Some historians have suggested that this was a fighting dog, such as the ones described in the tales of war from pagan Ireland.*

The only representation of a wolf in the Book of Kells, *folio 76v.*

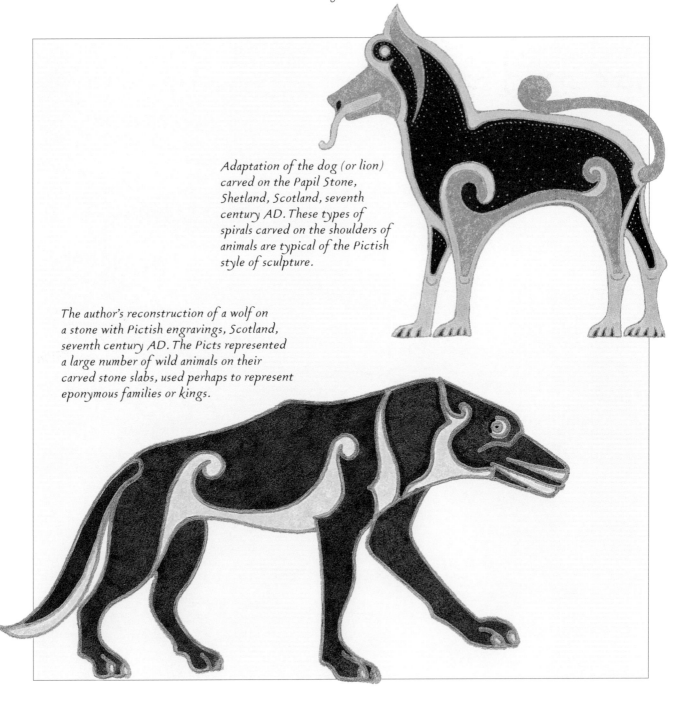

Adaptation of the dog (or lion) carved on the Papil Stone, Shetland, Scotland, seventh century AD. These types of spirals carved on the shoulders of animals are typical of the Pictish style of sculpture.

The author's reconstruction of a wolf on a stone with Pictish engravings, Scotland, seventh century AD. The Picts represented a large number of wild animals on their carved stone slabs, used perhaps to represent eponymous families or kings.

Dogs and wolves (continued)
Diversity of forms

Detail from the Book of Kells, *folio 48r. Greyhound chasing a hare.*

Wild boars and deer

Diversity of forms

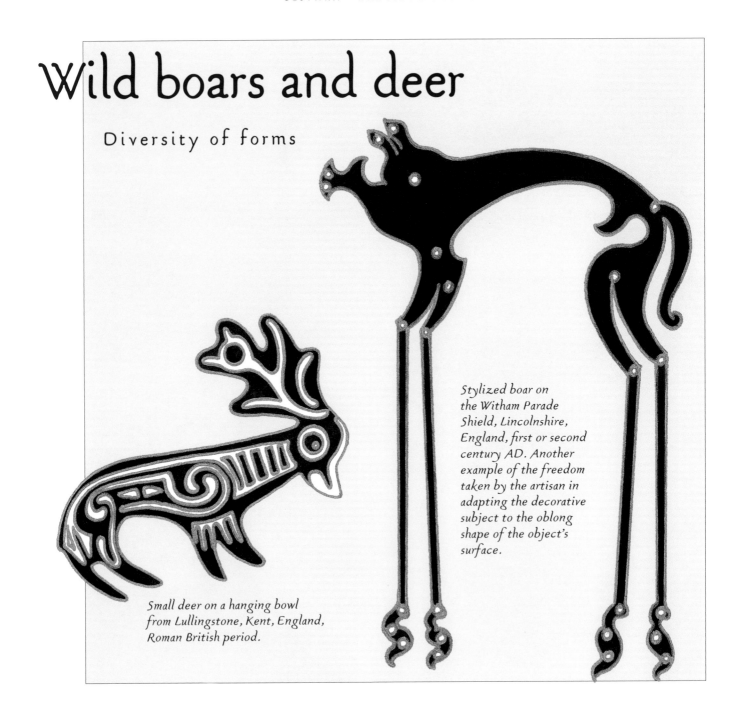

Stylized boar on the Witham Parade Shield, Lincolnshire, England, first or second century AD. Another example of the freedom taken by the artisan in adapting the decorative subject to the oblong shape of the object's surface.

Small deer on a hanging bowl from Lullingstone, Kent, England, Roman British period.

*Boar adorning a Gallo-Roman
statuette, Euffigneix, Haute-Marne,
France, first century BC.*

*Based on a bronze statuette of a boar, Bata,
Hungary, first century BC or AD. The Celts
often represented the boar enraged, its hair
standing on end, at the moment when it is about
to unleash its savage force.*

Deer

Diversity of forms

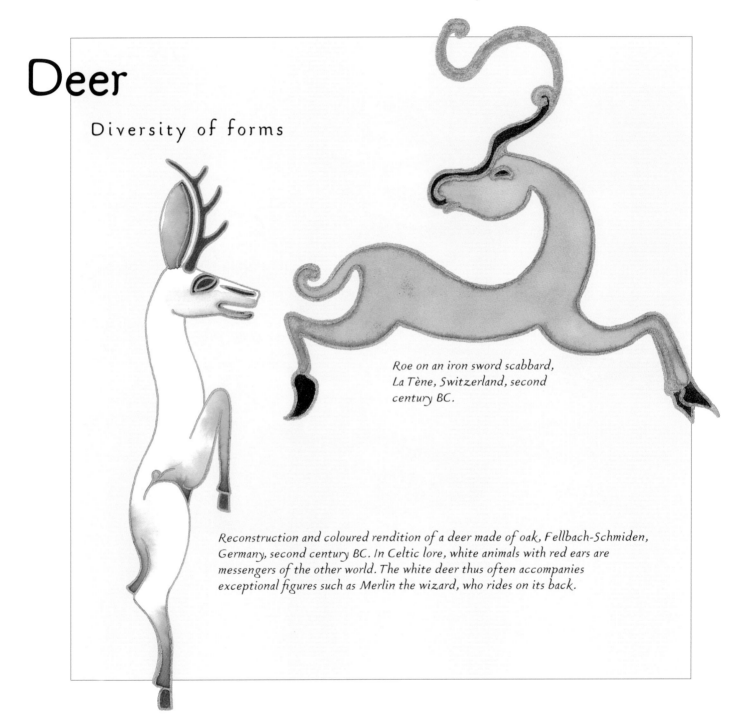

Roe on an iron sword scabbard, La Tène, Switzerland, second century BC.

Reconstruction and coloured rendition of a deer made of oak, Fellbach-Schmiden, Germany, second century BC. In Celtic lore, white animals with red ears are messengers of the other world. The white deer thus often accompanies exceptional figures such as Merlin the wizard, who rides on its back.

The only representation
of a deer in the Book of
Kells, *folio 302r.*

Deer sculpted
on a cross at Tibberaghny,
County Kilkenny, Ireland.

Horses

Diversity of forms

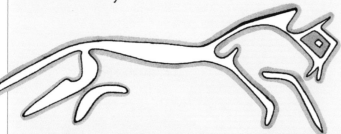

Detail from
the Gospel
book of St
Gatien, Irish
inspiration,
eighth
century AD.

Horse drawn in the chalky ground
(on a surface of around 100 m [328 ft]),
near Uffington, Oxfordshire, England,
first century BC. Amazingly, local
communities have maintained this figure
to this day.

Bronze horse
mask from
Stanwick,
Middlesex, England,
first century AD.
The extremely
stylized nature
of this mask is
reminiscent of certain
African objects.

Two sea horses on a
cross slab at Aberlemno,
Angus, Scotland, early
ninth century AD. The
waves of the ocean are
often compared in Celtic
poems to the sea horses
of the god Mananann
Mac Lir.

Mare on a silver coin from the region of Bratislava, Slovakia, ancient Celtic art. The stylization includes the most trivial details.

Horse drawing a cart on a gold coin attributed to the Turones tribe, middle Loire region, France, around 150 – 121 BC. The solar horse pulling the chariot of Apollo found on Greek stater coins inspired numerous Gaulish coins. The Gauls associated Apollo with Belenos.

Winged ox, symbol of St Luke, Book of Kells, folio 290r. The shimmering colours of the Book of Kells often astonish contemporary observers: one can only imagine the amazement and admiration that people in the early Middle Ages must have felt at such profusion of colour.

The ox of St Luke

Diversity of forms

Winged ox, symbol of St Luke,
Lindisfarne Gospels, folio 137v.

Ox of St Luke, Book of Durrow, *folio 124v. On this image, Irish artists omitted the wings usually attributed to the symbol of St Luke, and opted for a stylization decorated with dots and spirals. For the Irish, the presence of a spotted, striped or pure white cow in a herd was a symbol of prosperity and guaranteed the protection of the fairies.*

Cows and bulls

Diversity of forms

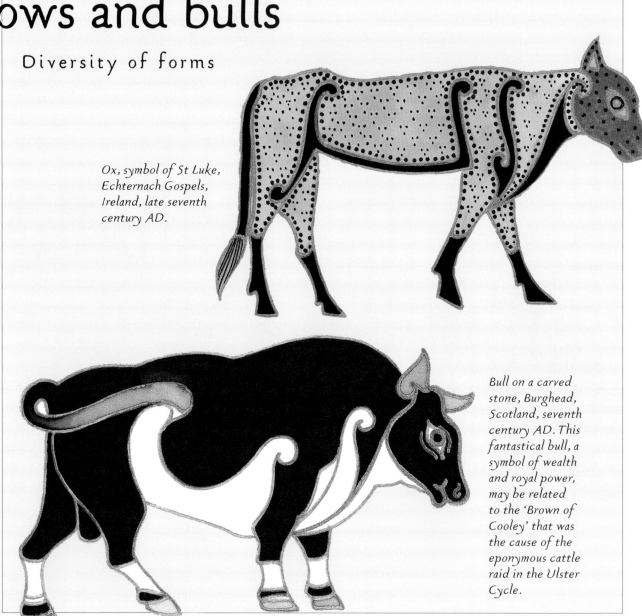

Ox, symbol of St Luke, Echternach Gospels, Ireland, late seventh century AD.

Bull on a carved stone, Burghead, Scotland, seventh century AD. This fantastical bull, a symbol of wealth and royal power, may be related to the 'Brown of Cooley' that was the cause of the eponymous cattle raid in the Ulster Cycle.

Winged ox, symbol of St Luke, Book of Armagh, Ireland, ninth century AD. On the wings of the animal, we can see the symbols of the other three evangelists: the eagle of St John, the lion of St Mark and the angel representing St Matthew.

The lion of St Mark

Diversity of forms

The author's adaptation of the lion, the symbol of St Mark, from the Book of Durrow, folio 191v. A resemblance to the animal that appears on the Papil Stone (see page 186) may be noted. In the early Middle Ages the lion was known to the Celts only from representations, which were often highly stylized.

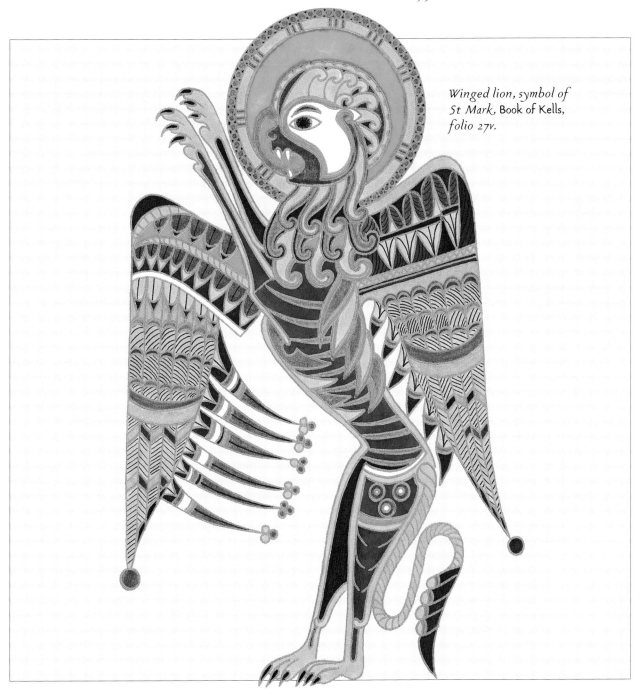

Winged lion, symbol of St Mark, Book of Kells, *folio 27v.*

*Lion, symbol of
St Mark, Harley
Manuscript, Ireland,
twelfth century.*

*Lion, symbol of St Mark,
Echternach Gospels, Ireland,
late seventh century AD.*

The lion of St Mark

Diversity of forms

Detail from the Book of Kells, *folio 129v. Another version of the lion of St Mark. These examples show the variety of interpretations of this animal, which was known to the Celts only from books.*

Lions and cats

Diversity of forms

Adaptation of the head of a lion, Book of Kells,
folio 292r. Lion heads are treated separately
in this book, as a decoration to crown columns
of interlace.

Coloured rendition of a feline face, on a capital in Tuam Cathedral, County Galway, Ireland, twelfth century.

Coloured rendition of a bronze head of a cat, Snowdon, Wales, first century AD. This strange handle of a bowl is also referred to as the 'Cheshire cat', after the magical cat that appears and disappears in Lewis Carroll's Alice in Wonderland.

Coloured rendition of a silenus (part human, part animal creature in Greek mythology) with a lion's face, the base of the handle of a bronze pitcher, Kleinaspergle, Germany, late fifth century BC. The first lions of Celtic art were inspired by Mediterranean decorative motifs.

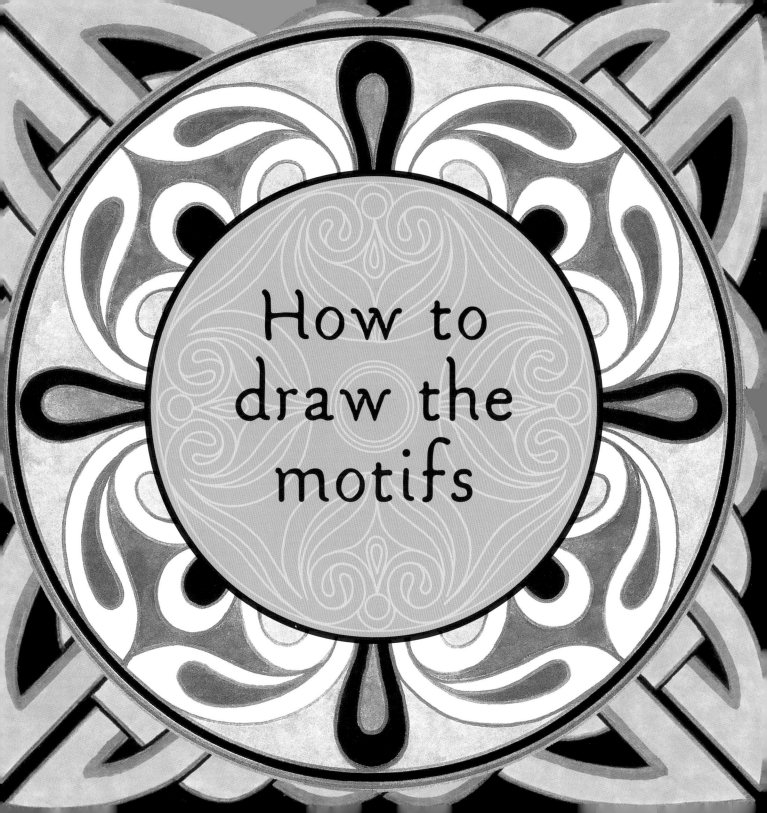

How to draw the motifs

see page 53

Three equidistant circles within a large circle

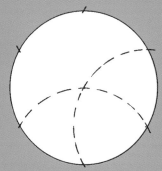

1 As when drawing a rose window, place six equidistant dots on the circle.

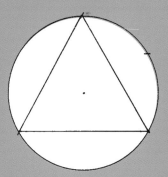

2 Draw an equilateral triangle.

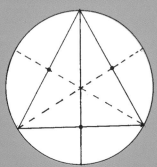

3 The intersection of the medians (lines linking the centre of the circle to one of the tips of the triangle) and the sides will become the centres of the subsequent circles.

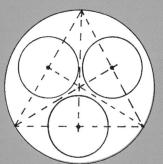

4 The circles starting from these centres will not overlap if we ensure their radius does not go beyond the medians.

A single spiral

see page 77

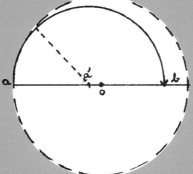

1 On the diameter of the circle, make a point a' wherever you wish. Draw a semicircle with radius [aa']. This gives us point b.

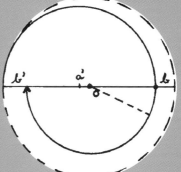

2 Draw a semicircle starting from centre O with radius [Ob]. This gives us point b'.

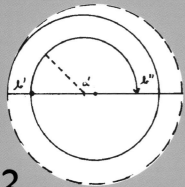

3 Draw a semicircle with radius [a'b']. This gives us b".

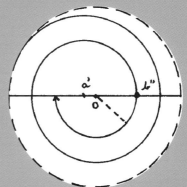

4 Continue in the same way, tracing semicircles alternating between the centres O and a'.

see page 65

A double spiral

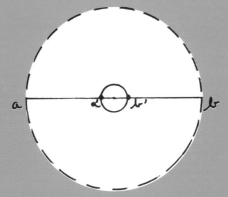

1 On diameter [ab] of the circle, use a compass to draw points a' and b', positioning them equidistant from the circle.

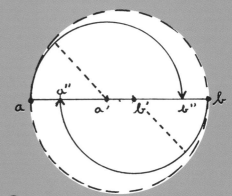

2 Draw semicircles: with centre a' and radius [aa'], by which you get point b"; with centre b' and radius [bb'], you get point a".

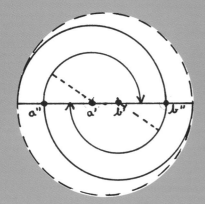

3 Draw the semicircle with centre a' and radius [a'a"], thus obtaining b"', and so on. This variation on the single spiral consists in alternating semicircles with centres a' and b'.

A triple spiral

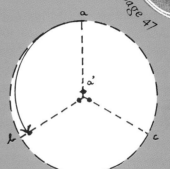

see page 47

1 Mark 3 equidistant points a, b and c on the circle. Draw the three radii of the circle from these points. Starting from the centre, draw another small circle. At the intersections of the small circle with the three radii, you get points a', b' and c', likewise equidistant.

2 Starting from a, draw the arc with centre a' and radius [aa']. A point of intersection is obtained between this arc and the following median.

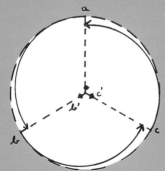

3 Repeat with the arcs with centre b' and c' and radius [bb'] [cc'], respectively.

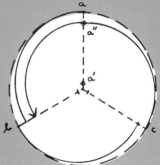

4 At the intersection of aa' and the arc starting from c, you get a". Now draw the arc starting from a", with centre a' and radius [a'a"]. Repeat for the two other arcs, and so on.

see page 39

The Ahenny triskel

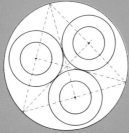

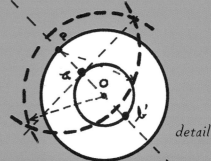

detail

1 Draw three equidistant circles as on page 206. Considering the radius of the large circle as measuring four units, draw circles with a radius of one unit, starting from the centre of each of the three circles.

2 Choose a circle. Starting from centre O and point a, draw two arcs with a radius greater than [Oa]; their intersection gives a straight line that intersects the median at b, the centre of the segment [Oa]. Draw a circle with centre O and radius [Ob], which intersects the median at b'. Repeat with the two other circles.

3 Draw the arcs with radius [Oa] and centre b and b'. Repeat with the two other circles. Then draw an intermediate circle as on the drawing. Connect the yin-yang figures to this circle.

4 Finish by creating a border of two lines around the drawing you have just made. You might want to use a compass for certain parts, using the various centres that have already been determined.

Triskel with birds

see page 54

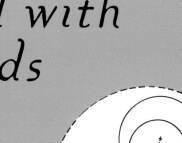

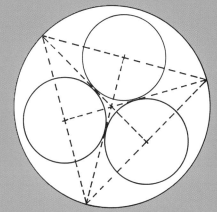

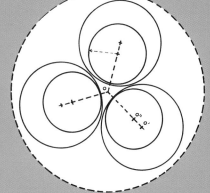

1 Draw the three equidistant circles as on page 206. Consider the radius of the large circle as measuring four units.

2 Draw the circles tangent to the first three, with a radius of one unit each, the centres of which are located on the medians connecting the centre of the large circle to the centres of the three equidistant circles.

3 Draw the heads of the birds. Then, using the drawings thus obtained, link the whole thing freehand to obtain the triskel. Erase any unnecessary lines.

see page 89

The Waldalgesheim interlace

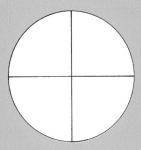

1 With a pencil, draw a circle and its two perpendicular diameters.

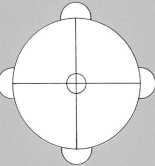

2 Draw a small central circle starting from the centre, and four arcs with a larger radius, with centres at the intersection of the large circle and the diameters.

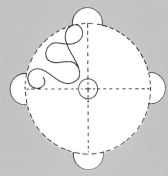

3 Draw the central line for the interlace.

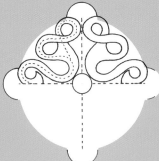

4 Draw the ribbon of the interlace along the central line. Using the diameters, reproduce the interlace in a symmetrical pattern. Repeat with the two other axes. Use felt pens for the final drawing, and erase the construction lines.

see page 92

Chalice with rinceaux

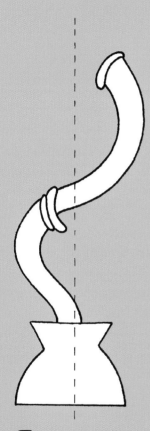

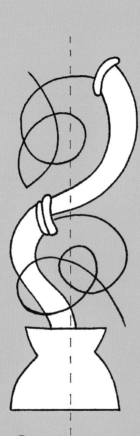

1 With a pencil, draw a vertical axis, the chalice and the central stock.

2 Draw the central lines of the secondary stems.

3 Following these lines, draw the ribbon of the secondary stems and their foliage. Go back over the outlines with black felt pen, following the rule of 'over-under', and then erase the construction lines.

An Irish cross

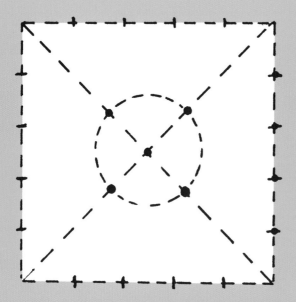 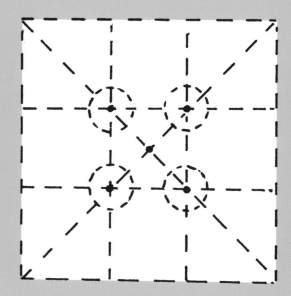

1 With a pencil, draw a square with sides five units in length and its diagonals. Then draw a circle with a radius of one unit, taking as the centre the intersection of the diagonals of the square. This circle intersects the diagonals at four points.

2 Draw four circles, each with a radius of half a unit, taking as the centre the points marked on the diagonals. Then, draw two horizontal and two vertical dotted lines through the centres of the small circles.

see page 61

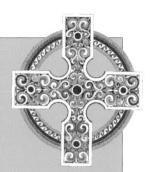

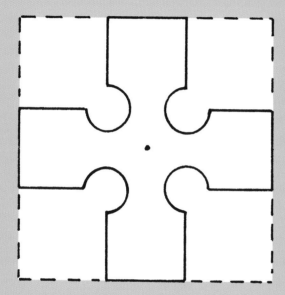

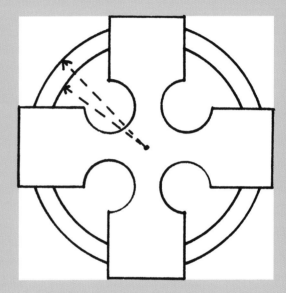

3 Go back over the lines of the cross with a felt pen, as on the diagram. You may, at this stage, extend the vertical axis of the cross. Let it dry.

4 With a soft eraser, remove any unnecessary lines. From the centre of the first circle, draw the arcs between the branches of the cross. Go back over the arcs with a black felt pen.

The diagonal interlace of Britford

see page 128

1 With a pencil, on a square with sides of 15 cm (6 in), draw the medians. Draw diagonal lines across the square at 1 cm intervals. Using this grid, draw the first triangular outline.

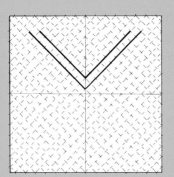

2 Extend the ribbon of the triangle as on the diagram.

3 Following the grid, draw the loop.

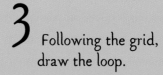

4 Taking as the centre the point where the diagonal lines intersect, reproduce the same design by rotating it 90°. In this way, repeat the basic interlace three times. Go back over the drawing in felt pen and erase the grid lines.

The dog from the Gospels of Lindisfarne

see page 135

1 With a pencil, draw the body of the dog.

2 Draw the central line of the tail and the ear.

3 Following this line, draw the ribbon of the interlace. Follow the rule of 'over-under'. Go over the outlines with a felt pen and then erase the construction lines.

Interlaced dogs

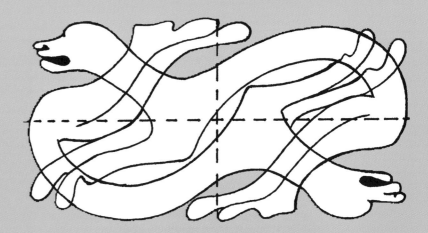

I With the help of two axes, draw the outlines of the two dogs.

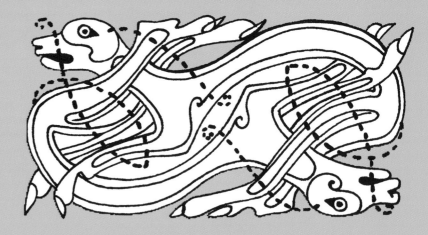

2 Draw the outlines and clarify the design with due care for the intersections; with a dotted line draw the tails and the ears.

see page 134

3 Clarify the whole drawing with due care for the intersections and following the 'over-under' rule of interlace.

The serpents from inside the

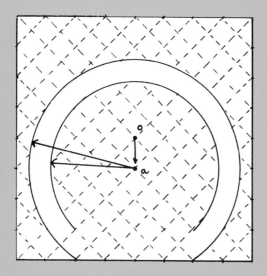

I With a pencil, draw a square with sides eight units in length. Draw the diagonals to find the centre, o. Now draw a diagonal grid across the square. Under the centre o of the square, take a point a. Draw two arcs centred on a, the first with a radius of five units in length along the diagonal that passes through point a, and the other with a radius of four units in length.

2 Extend the resulting 'ribbon' into a cross, as shown above.

cross of the Book of Kells

see page 136

3 From point a, draw two new arcs, one with a radius of three units and one with a radius of two units.

4 Extend the 'ribbons' as shown. To complete the motif as on page 136, add small ribbons freehand and follow the 'over-under' rule of interlace. Go back over the drawing in felt pen; let it dry and then erase any unnecessary lines.

King Solomon's knot

see page 119

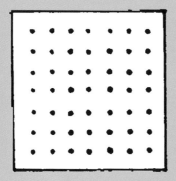

1 Draw a square with eight-unit sides. Create a grid. At the intersections of the grid, mark the points.

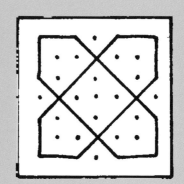

2 Connect the dots as follows, without taking the interlace into account.

3 Following the lines that you have drawn, draw the bands as shown, using the intersection points as a guide.

4 Fill the enclosed spaces and finish drawing the interlace by following the 'over-under' rule.

Meigle's knot

see page 111

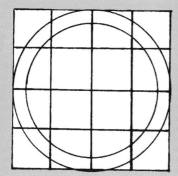

I Draw a square with sides of four units, and using its centre, draw two concentric circles. Fill the square with a grid.

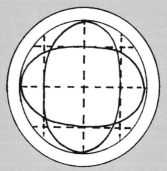

2 Using this grid, draw the first lines of the knot structure freehand.

3 Following these lines, draw the bands freehand, without taking into account the 'over-under' rule.

4 Fill in the enclosed spaces, and finish the interlace following the 'over-under' rule.

see page 164

A Welsh cross

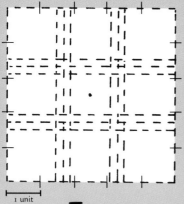

1 unit

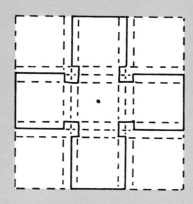

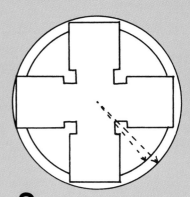

1 With a pencil, draw a square with five-unit sides. Draw two perpendicular lines through the centres of the sides of the square. Now draw parallel lines on each side of these segments, at intervals of 0.8 of a unit. On each side of these lines, draw new parallel segments at 0.2 of a unit.

2 Go back over the lines of the cross in felt pen as shown. Let it dry, then erase any unnecessary lines with a soft eraser.

3 Finish the design by drawing a disc or a ring, starting from the centre of the cross (at the intersection of the perpendicular lines drawn in step 1, and passing through the centres of the sides of the square).

The arrows from the crosses of Galmorgan and Kilfenora

see page 163

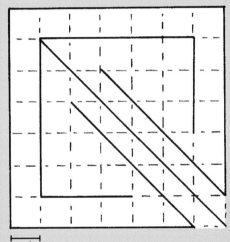

1 unit

1 With a pencil, draw grid lines in a square with sides seven units in length. Draw the diagonal lines as shown and continue the central diagonal, following the perimeter along the inner square.

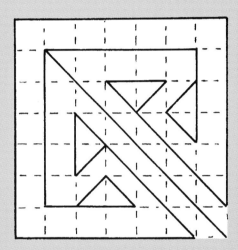

2 Finish the design by drawing the isosceles triangles. If you want to draw the crosses of Galmorgan and Kilfenora, reproduce the drawing three times symmetrically along an axis, starting at the right side of the first square drawn. Go back over the drawing in felt pen; let it dry and then erase any unnecessary lines.

A labyrinth
taken from the Book of Kells

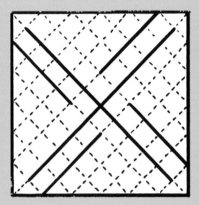

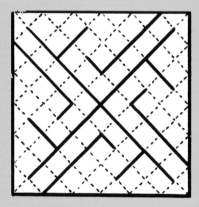

1 Draw a square of 6 x 6 units and create a diagonal grid. Then draw the first diagonal lines.

2 Continue drawing the extension of these diagonal lines, and you will get the first right angles.

3 Finally, extend the parallel lines to the sides to finish the edges, and fill in the triangles this creates.

A band with a simple labyrinth, taken from the Book of Kells

see page 167

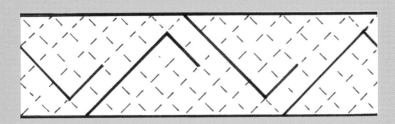

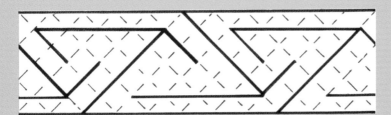

1 Draw a band three units in width, and fill with a diagonal grid, as before. Draw the first equidistant diagonal lines as well, extending them by small right angles.

2 Draw the lines parallel to the sides of the band, starting with the angles drawn previously. These lines end in acute angles.

3 Fill in as shown, with two small isosceles triangles of the same size, using for their base the parallel lines drawn in step 2.

see page 161

A band with a more complex labyrinth

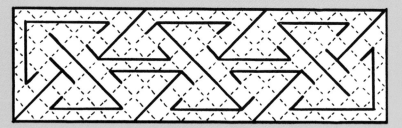

1 Draw a band with grid lines four or five units in width and sixteen in length. The first diagonals end in right angles.

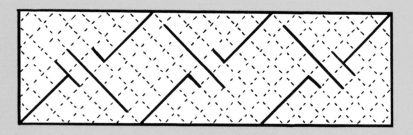

2 Draw the lines parallel to the edges of the band.

3 Fill in the triangles.

A labyrinth
taken from the Book of Kells *see page 169*

1 Create oblique grid lines in a square with sides of ten units. Draw the first diagonals.

2 Extend the diagonals. Use the central point as the axis of symmetry.

3 Draw a border of half a unit, connecting the angles you have just created. Fill in the enclosed spaces. Finish the spirals with small right angles.

Remarkable carpet pages p.231
Major dates p.231
Map and chronology p.232
Glossary p.234
Bibliography p.236

Remarkable carpet pages

BOOK OF KELLS

folio 202v, the Temptation
folio 7v, the Virgin and Child
folio 27v, symbols of the four evangelists
folio 28v, portrait of St Matthew
folio 29r, Mt 1:1 Liber generationis
folio 32v, portrait of Christ
folio 33r, cross with eight medallions (opposite)
folio 34r, page with Chi-Ro, or monogram of Christ
(Christi autem generatio)
folio 114r, the kiss of Judas
folio 129v, symbols of the four evangelists
folio 130r, beginning of the Gospel of St Mark
folio 188r, beginning of the Gospel of St Luke
folio 290v, symbols of the four evangelists
folio 291r, portrait of St John holding his writing
instruments
folio 292r, beginning of the Gospel of St John

BOOK OF DURROW

folio 1v, folio 3v, folio 21v, folio 84v,
folio 85v, folio 124v, folio 125v, folio 191v,
folio 192v, folio 248r.

LINDISFARNE GOSPELS

folio 2v, folio 3r, folio 25v, folio 26v,
folio 27r, folio 29r, folio 93v, folio 94v,
folio 95r, folio 137v, folio 138v, folio 139r,
folio 209v, folio 210v, folio 211r.

Major dates

ILLUMINATED BOOKS MENTIONED IN THE INTRODUCTION

Echternach Gospels,
end of the seventh century AD (closely
related to the Irish illuminated manuscripts)

St Chad (or Lichfield) Gospels,
beginning of the eighth century AD

St Gall Gospel book, eighth century AD

St Gatien Gospel book, eighth century AD

Gospel book of Mac Regol, ninth century AD

Book of Mac Durnan, ninth century AD

Book of Dimma, eighth century AD

Book of Armagh, ninth century AD

Harley manuscript, twelfth century

In addition to this list, there are other
sources more infrequently cited in this book.

ATLANTIC
OCEAN

Shetland Islands

Hebrides
Islands

Orkney Islands

Scotland

NORWAY

SWEDEN

Lake
Vänern

Lake
Vättern

FINLAND

Gulf of Finland

ESTONIA

Gulf of
Riga

LATVIA

LITHUANIA

R

NORTH
SEA

UNITED
KINGDOM

IRELAND

Irish
Sea

British
Isles

DENMARK

BALTIC SEA

Elbe

Vistula

Oder

POLAND

BELARUS

Land's End

Thames

Channel

Strait of Calais

THE
NETHERLANDS

BELGIUM

Meuse

Rhine

Elbe

GERMANY

Vistula

Carpathians

Dnieper

UKR

Seine

LUXEMBOURG

Danube

CZECH
REPUBLIC

Dniester

FRANCE

Loire

LIECHTENSTEIN

Inn

AUSTRIA
Hallstatt

SLOVAKIA

Great Plain of
Hungary

Danube

MOLDOVA

Massif
Central

Jura

Rhine

SWITZERLAND
La Tène

4.810

Rhône

Alps

Pò

MONACO

HUNGARY

Drava

Drava

ROMANIA

SLOVENIA

Sava

Cape
Finisterre

Bay of
Biscay

Garonne

Pyrenees

Cantabrian Mountains

Gulf of
Lyon

Ligurian
Sea

SAN
MARINO

CROATIA

BOSNIA AND
HERZEGOVINA

SERBIA

BULGARIA

Bosporus

Douro

PORTUGAL

SPAIN

Ebro

ANDORRA

Corsica

VATICAN CITY

MONTENEGRO

KOSOVO

Balkans

Sea of
Marmara

Tagus

Guadiana

Sierra Morena

Sierra Nevada

Balearic Islands

Sardinia

Tyrrhenian
Sea

Apennines

ADRIATIC SEA

Strait of Otranto

ITALY

MACEDONIA

ALBANIA

Pindhos Mountains

Dardanelles

Aegean Sea

TUR

Strait of
Gibraltar

MEDITERRANEAN SEA

Sicily

Strait
of Messina

Ionian
Sea

Ionian Islands

GREECE

MOROCCO

ALGERIA

TUNISIA

MALTA

MEDITERRANEAN SEA

Crete

Hallstatt cu
(eighth cen

Celtic territ
La Tène civi

Celtic territ
of its expan

Retreat of C
Roman Emp

● Major archa

Chronology

PRINCIPAL DATES IN THE ANCIENT CIVILIZATIONS OF EUROPE

The Paleolithic period: ends around the tenth millennium BC
The Neolithic era: ninth to third millennium BC
Bronze Age: from the second millennium BC
Iron Age: from the first millennium BC
Cycladic civilization: from the third millennium BC
Minoan civilization (Crete): 2700 – 1200 BC
Mycenaean civilization (Greece): 1700 – 1200 BC
Archaic Greece: ninth to sixth century BC
Geometric period in Greece: ninth to eighth century BC
Classical Greece: fifth to fourth century BC
Etruscan civilization: late eighth to third century BC
Roman Empire: 27 BC – AD 476
Byzantine Empire: AD 359 – 1453

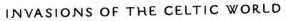

INVASIONS OF THE CELTIC WORLD

Anglo-Saxons: fifth and sixth centuries AD
Viking invasions: eighth to eleventh century AD
Anglo-Norman conquests: twelfth century AD

THE DIFFERENT STYLES AND PERIODS OF CELTIC ART
(place names are contemporary)

Hallstatt period: eighth to fifth century BC, first Iron Age, central Europe
La Tène period: fifth to first century BC, second Iron Age, continental Europe
Insular Celtic art: fifth century BC to twelfth century AD, in Ireland and Britain
Irish Golden Age: fifth to twelfth century AD
Celtic revival: mid-nineteenth century in Ireland, Scotland, Wales and Armorican Brittany

Glossary

ANATOLIA • region of central Turkey.

ARCHETYPE • according to the theory of C.G. Jung, the universal structure or model that appears in myths and in the products of the human imagination.

ARTS AND CRAFTS • movement led by William Morris at the end of the nineteenth century, aiming to renew the decorative arts in England.

ASKLEPIOS (AESCULAPIUS) • ancient Greek / Roman god of medicine.

BAO PING • Chinese ornament in the form of a vase, which is one of the eight auspicious signs in Buddhism.

BASILICA • a Roman building in the form of a large rectangular hall ending in an apse, the first architectural model for Christian churches.

BUCRANE • Mediterranean ornament in the form of an emaciated ox skull or head.

CADUCEUS • a winged laurel or olive staff entwined with two interlaced serpents, the attribute of Hermes.

CARPET PAGE • a page on parchment in Celtic illuminated books, covered with a particularly complex set of Celtic motifs.

CHANCEL RAILOR SCREEN • low railing or screen separating the choir from the nave in early Christian churches.

CHEVRON • decorative motif in the shape of a V.

COPT • Egyptian or Ethiopian Christian.

CORIOLIS FORCE • centrifugal force, caused by the rotation of the earth, which affects all liquids in motion on the planet.

DAOISM • Chinese religion based on popular beliefs and the writings of Laozi, according to whom the universe is governed by an impersonal principle of order and unity, the Dao.

FILIGREE • gold- or silverwork made of interlaced and soldered metal threads.

FRACTALS • curve or surface created according to the rules of internal homothety, or iteration. The shape of each of the elements making up the fractal is similar to the shape of the whole.

GNOSIS • philosophical and religious doctrine that studies the mysteries of God and creation.

GOSPEL BOOK • a liturgical book containing all the passages of the Gospel read in the course of the Eucharistic celebration.

GREEK KEY • ancient ornamental motif consisting of a broken straight line that bends in right angles and reverses direction, forming a decorative border (also known as Greek fret).

GUILLOCHE • engraved decoration made up of undulating lines that intersect in a regular pattern.

HIBERNO-SAXON • combining the characteristics of Irish and Saxon cultures.

HIBERNO-VIKING • combining the characteristics of the Irish and Viking cultures.

HITTITES • an Indo-European people that established a powerful civilization in central Anatolia in the earliest antiquity.

INDO-EUROPEAN • initially, a linguistic term designating several languages of Europe and western Asia, which are thought to have had a common origin. The term is applied, by extension, to civilizations that speak these Indo-European languages.

INFLECTION • change in direction of the curvature of a plane curve.

ISIS • Egyptian goddess, the 'paredra' (consort) of Osiris, she was the object of a mystery cult in Antiquity.

KRATER • a large Greek vase with a wide opening and two handles, in which water or wine was kept.

LYRE • decorative motif made up of symmetrical S shapes.

MEANDER • ancient decorative motif closely resembling the Greek key, made up of chains of U shapes.

MOIRAE • implacable goddesses of fate in Greek mythology.

NATURA NATURANS • a medieval scholastic term applied to nature considered in its act of creation.

OSIRIS • Egyptian god of the dead, the judge of souls in the afterlife.

PALMETTE • stylized motif, the shape of which resembles a bouquet of comma shapes, and is reminiscent of certain types of palm leaves.

PARCAE • Roman goddesses equivalent to the Greek Moirae.

PELTA • classical ornamental motif shaped like a fan whose two upper points are rolled up into a spiral.

PICTS • an ancient tribe living in what is now Scotland, before the arrival of the Scots.

PURNA KUMBHA • in the Indian decorative repertoire, a motif representing a ceremonial vase from which a bouquet of plants springs forth.

PYTHAGORAS • a Greek philosopher and mathematician of the sixth century BC, who considered that numbers are the source and origin of all things.

RINCEAUX • decorative borders or strips featuring stylized vines with leaves and often flowers and fruit.

ROUNDEL • ornamental motif in the form of a small wheel.

SCHOLASTICISM • academic study and teaching of philosophy and theology in the Middle Ages, based on an interpretation of the Aristotelian tradition.

STAMNOI • a vase with a small horizontal handle and a narrow mouth, used to store wine.

SUFISM • a mystical movement within Islam that appeared in the eighth century AD.

SWASTIKA • from Sanskrit, meaning 'small sign of well-being'. Symbol of well-being that is particularly widely developed in the Hindu, Buddhist and Jain visual repertoire; an equal-armed cross, whose branches are oriented towards the left.

TANTRIC • relating to the ritual and magical practices of Hinduism and Buddhism.

TESSERA • small square of ceramic tile, or sometimes semi-precious stone, used to make mosaics.

TETRAMORPH • in the Old Testament, the 'four living creatures' pulling the chariot in the vision of Ezekiel (Ezekiel 1: 1-14).

TORSADE • decorative motif imitating two intertwined cables.

TOTEM • animal or plant considered to be the ancestor of an ethnic group.

TRISKEL • Celtic radiating motif made up of three equidistant spirals that seem to be propelled by a gyratory movement.

ULATES • the inhabitants of Ulster, northern Irish Kingdom.

YIN-YANG • a circle divided into two comma shapes, with a white disc inside the black comma and a black one in the white comma shape. The symbol, of Daoist origin, describes the principle of equilibrium between the masculine Yang force and the feminine Yin force.

Bibliography

CELTIC MOTIFS, METHODS OF CONSTRUCTION

Davis, Courtney. 101 *Celtic Crosses*, David & Charles Publishers, 2004.

—. 101 *Celtic Knotwork Designs*. F&W Publishers, 2004.

—. 101 *Celtic Spirals*, F&W Publishers, 2005.

Le Roux, Charles. *Ornementation bretonne*. Coop Breizh, 1984.

Meehan, Aidan. *Celtic Design: A Beginner's Manual, Knotwork, Illuminated Letters*. Thames and Hudson, 2007.

—. *Celtic Design: Animal Patterns*. Thames and Hudson, 1992.

—. *Celtic Design: The Dragon and the Griffin*, Thames and Hudson, 1995.

—. *Celtic Design: Maze Patterns*, Thames and Hudson, 1994.

—. *Celtic Design: Spiral Patterns*. Thames and Hudson, 1993.

—. *Celtic Design: The Tree of Life*. Thames and Hudson, 1996.

Stead, Ian and Karen Hughes. *Early Celtic Designs*. British Museum Press, 1997.

Wilson, Eva. *Early Medieval Designs*. British Museum Press, 2000.

Zaczek, Iain. *Celtic Art and Design*. Moyer Bell, 1996.

CELTIC ART

Allen, J. Romilly. *Celtic Crosses of Wales*. J.M.F. Bookfinding Service, repr. 1989.

Brown, Michelle. *The Lindisfarne Gospels*. University of Toronto Press, 2003.

Les Celtes, Editions EDDL, 2001.

Crawford, H.S. *Irish Carved Ornament*. Mercier Press, 1980.

Cunliffe, Barry. *The Celtic World*. St Martin's Press, 1993.

Davis, Courtney. *The Irish School, Celtic Illumination*. Thames and Hudson, 1998.

Duval, Paul-Marie. *Les Celtes*. Gallimard (L'Univers des Formes), 1977.

—. *Monnaies gauloises*. Editions Hermann, 1987.

Eluère, Christiane. *L'Or des Celtes*. Fribourg: Office du livre, 1987.

Green, Miranda. *The Celtic World*. Routledge, 1995.

Harbison, Peter. *Irish High Crosses*. The Boyne Valley Honey Cy, 1994.

—. *Medieval Art in Ireland*. London, 1999.

Laing, Lloyd and Jennifer. *The Art of the Celts*. Thames and Hudson, 1992.

Le Couédic D. and J.-Y. Veillard, eds. *Ar Seiz Breur*. Terre de Brume, 2000.

Meehan, Bernard. *The Book of Durrow*. Dublin: Town House, 1996.

—. *The Book of Kells*. Thames and Hudson, 1995.

Megaw, Ruth and Vincent. *Celtic Art*. Thames and Hudson, 2001.

Müller, Felix. *Art of the Celts*. Mercatorfonds/ Thames and Hudson, 2009.

Pineau, Serj. *Magie de l'art celtique ancien*. Coop Breizh, 2005.

Zaczek, Iain. *Celtic Art and Design*. Moyer Bell, 1996.

HISTORY OF DECORATION

Buci-Glucksmann, Christine. *Philosophie de l'ornement*. Ed. Galilée, 2008.

Gimbutas, Marija. *The Language of the Goddess*. Harper and Row, 1989.

Jones, Owen. *The Grammar of Ornament*. L'aventurine, 2001 (original ed. 1910).

Petrie, Flinders. *3000 Decorative Patterns of the Ancient World*. Dover, 1986.

Thomas, N.L. *Irish Symbols of 3500 B.C.* Mercier Press, 1988, repr. 1994.

Wilson, Eva. *8000 Years of Ornament*. British Museum Press, 1994.

SIGNS, SYMBOLS AND MYTHS

Alleau, René. *La Science des symboles*. Payot, 1976.

Benoist, Luc. *Signes, symboles et mythes* (Que sais-je ?). PUF, 1975.

Burckhardt, Titus. *Principes et méthodes de l'art sacré*. Dervy, 1995.

Coomaraswamy, A.K. *Christian and Oriental Philosophy of Art*. M. Manoharlal Publishers, 2008.

—. *Figures of Speech or Figures of Thought*. M. Manoharlal Publishers, 1981.

Cotterell, Arthur. *Celtic Mythology*. Lorenz, 2000.

Daniélou, Jean. *Primitive Christian Symbols* (trans. D. Attwater). Burns & Oates, 1964.

Davis, Courtney. *Celtic Beasts*. Blandford, 1999.

Eliade, Mircea. *Images and Symbols* (trans. Philip Mairet). Harvill Press, 1961.

Ghyka, Matila. *Le Nombre d'or*. Gallimard, 1931.

Guénon, René. *Symboles de la science sacrée*. Gallimard, 1962.

—. *Le Symbolisme de la croix*. Ed. Guy Trédaniel, 1996.

Heinz, Sabine. *Les Symboles des Celtes*. Ed. Guy Trédaniel, 1998.

Jolif, Thierry. *Symboles celtiques*. Editions Pardès, 2004.

Kervella, Divi. *Emblèmes et symboles des Bretons et des Celtes*. Coop Breizh, 1998.

Mackillop, James. *Dictionary of Celtic Mythology*. Oxford University Press, 2004.

Pastoureau, Michel. *Une histoire symbolique du Moyen Âge occidental*. Le Seuil, 2004.

Purce, Jill. *The Mystic Spiral*. Thames and Hudson, 1974.

Streit, Jakob. *Sun and Cross*. Floris Books, 1984.

Thomas, N.L. *Irish Symbols of 3500 B.C.* Mercier Press, 1988.

Note to the reader

The motifs chosen for this book have been classified according to the traditional four major groups of Celtic motifs: spirals, interlace, labyrinths and bestiary. The majority have been identified and dated according to current practice in order to make it possible for readers to look up the originals in books on Celtic art. Brief, judicious commentaries explain the particularities of the chosen motifs.

Certain motifs, in particular elements from crosses or from carpet pages, have been adapted to the square format of the book. Others are line drawings based on motifs that adorn jewellery or ceramics. Finally, some are the author's own designs, based on the principles of construction of traditional motifs.

The motifs were drawn with pencil on Canson 224g paper and were then finished with metallic ink, gouache, watercolours and brush-tip pens. The colours are generally based for the most part on the colour combinations found in Irish illuminated books.

David Balade

Find David Balade's creations at www.keris-artshop.com

Photographic credits

Endpapers: *Book of Durrow*, carpet page folio 3v. Trinity College, Dublin, Ireland. © AKG-images. Inside of endpapers: *Lindisfarne Gospels*, folio 26v. British Library, London, England. © AKG-images / British Library. • p. 4: Kilmainham Brooch. National Museum of Ireland, Dublin, Ireland. © Boltin Picture Library / Bridgeman Giraudon. • p. 4: Detail of the Battersea Shield. British Museum, London, England. © Bridgeman Giraudon. • p. 6: Schwarzenbach Bowl. National Museums, Berlin, Germany. © Bridgeman Giraudon. • p. 7: Bronze knot. Private collection. © Heini Schneebeli / Bridgeman Giraudon. • p. 9: First page of the Lichfield Gospels. Lichfield Cathedral, Staffordshire, England. © Bridgeman Giraudon. • p. 10: Gospel of St John, taken from the *Book of Kells*. Trinity College, Dublin, Ireland. © Bridgeman Giraudon. • p. 11: Portrait of St John, taken from the *Book of Kells*. Trinity College, Dublin, Ireland. © Bridgeman Giraudon.

CHAPTER ON SPIRALS AND TRISKELS • p. 12: Vague. © Valéry Hache. • p. 13: Bronze mirror back. Desborough, Northamptonshire, England. © AKG-images / Erich Lessing. • p. 15: Vase illustrated with octopus design. Ashmolean Museum, Oxford, England. © Bridgeman Giraudon. • p. 16: Detail of a bronze handle. Archaeological Museum of Châtillon-sur-Seine, France. © Bridgeman Giraudon. • p. 17: Bronze shield. Archaeological Museum, Olympia, Greece. Collection of ancient art and architecture. © Bridgeman Giraudon. • p. 18: Romano-Celtic bronze appliqué. Private collection. © Heini Schneebeli / Bridgeman Giraudon.

CHAPTER ON INTERLACE • p. 78: Tree of Ponthus. Forest of Brocéliande, Brittany, France. © Emmanuel Berthier. • p. 79: Pictish stone of Collieburn. Dunrobin Castle Museum, Golspie, Scotland. Collection of ancient art and architecture. © Bridgeman Giraudon. • p. 81: Silver-plated side of the shrine of St Patrick's Bell. National Museum of Ireland, Dublin. © Boltin Picture Library / Bridgeman Giraudon. • p. 82: Gold brooch. National Museums of Scotland. © Bridgeman Giraudon. • p. 84: Amulet of Isis Knot. © RMN / Hervé Lewandowski.

CHAPTER ON LABYRINTHS • p. 150: Tascon, Morbihan, France. © Emmanuel Berthier. • pp. 151 and 155: Mosaic floor. Conimbriga, Coimbra, Portugal. © AKG-images / Erich Lessing. • p. 156: Detail of a Roman mosaic of Theseus. © AKG-images / Erich Lessing.

CHAPTER ON BESTIARY • p. 174: Illuminated page from the *Book of Kells*. Trinity College, Dublin, Ireland. © AKG-images. • p. 175: A man, possibly a god, riding a dolphin. Gundestrup Cauldron, second century BC. National Museum of Denmark, Copenhagen. © AKG-images / Erich Lessing. • p. 176: Relief on the Gundestrup Cauldron. National Museum of Denmark, Copenhagen. © AKG-images / Erich Lessing. • p. 177: Bronze fibula. Private collection. © Heini Schneebeli / Bridgeman Giraudon. • p. 178: Bronze statuette. Saarland, Germany. © AKG-images / Erich Lessing. • p. 179: Cernunnos, antlered Celtic god. © AKG-images / Erich Lessing. • p. 181: Gospel of St Matthew, *Book of Kells*. Trinity College, Dublin, Ireland. © Bridgeman Giraudon.

CHAPTER ON HOW TO DRAW THE MOTIFS AND APPENDICES • p. 204: Gilded disc with decoration in S and spiral patterns. Cabinet of Medallions, Auvers-sur-Oise, Yvelines, France. © AKG-images / Pietro Baguzzi. • p. 230: *Book of Kells*. Trinity College, Dublin, Ireland. © AKG-images.

© 2010 Editions Ouest-France – Edilarge SA, Rennes
Author: David Balade • Editor of the French edition: Catherine Dandres Franck
Cartography: Patrick Mérienne • Graphic design: Isabelle Chêne
Published by Vivays Publishing Ltd • www.vivays-publishing.com
This edition © 2011 Vivays Publishing Ltd
English translation: Monica Sandor for LocTeam, Barcelona
Typesetting and text editing: LocTeam, Barcelona
Cover design: Ute Conin, Cologne
Printed in France by Polina
ISBN 978-1-908126-13-9